∞

ALSO BY HEATHER HAVRILESKY

What If This Were Enough?

How to Be a Person in the World

Disaster Preparedness

Foreverland

On the Divine Tedium of Marriage

Heather Havrilesky

An Imprint of HarperCollinsPublishers

The events and experiences detailed here are all true and have been faithfully rendered as I have remembered them, to the best of my ability. Some names and identifying details have been changed to protect the privacy of the individuals involved.

Though conversations come from my recollection of them, they are not written to represent word-for-word documentation. I've retold them in a way that evokes the feeling and meaning of what was said, in keeping with the mood and spirit of the event.

FIRST EDITION

Designed by Paula Russell Szafranski

Infinity symbol © Nataliia Tosun / Shutterstock.com

Library of Congress Cataloging-in-Publication Data has been applied for.

ISBN 978-0-06-298446-3

22 23 24 25 26 LSC 10 9 8 7 6 5 4 3 2 1

FOR BILL

CONTENTS

PART I

1

Beginning

Every book about marriage is also a book about mortality, since the success of any marriage is defined not by happiness or good fortune but by death. The assignment, after all, is to stay together until you die. Once one spouse perishes, the marriage has succeeded. Death signals victory.

Only an optimistic fool would declare victory before reaching the finish line. That's what makes weddings such dark comedies. What's more entertaining and ominous than watching two naive souls sign a binding contract without understanding the fine print? Most engaged couples bumble onto the marital bullet train without even knowing where it's headed. *All that matters is that we'll be together,* they whisper to each other. Forever is two immortal elves, sipping pink champagne by a burbling stream, then exploring the wild, gorgeous woods around them in everlasting harmony. Forever is set in New Zealand, not New Jersey.

Muddling through the first year of marriage has a way of turning New Zealand back into New Jersey, changing pink champagne into a juice box, and transforming two immortal elves into lumpy humans with a rapidly approaching expiration date.

Even after many satisfying years together, married life has an uncanny way of making even the most buoyant soul feel like a fool and a failure repeatedly. It's a feature, not a bug. Marriage is designed to break you. You will forget everything you knew before. You will tremble under the weight of your own shortcomings. Sure, you might bounce back and proclaim yourself lucky and declare your marriage happy and become the masochist your marriage wants you to be. But you'll still wake up plenty of mornings wondering why you signed on to drag this wretched, snoring heap of meat with you everywhere you go until the day you die.

And once you're married and therefore a true masochist, you'll realize that all of these sensations are part of the delicious tedium of matrimony. I wrote this book to explore that tedium, along with everything else that marriage brings: the feeling of safety, the creeping darkness, the raw fear and suspense of growing older together, the tiny repeating irritations, the rushes of love, the satisfactions of companionship, the unexpected rage of recognizing that your partner will probably never change. And in writing this book, I discovered new layers within my marriage and myself, haunting and chaotic, wretched and unlovable.

We talk about marriage like it's just something people do, no big deal. We pretend that once you're married, you're either happy or unhappy, a binary system, on or off. But the truth is so much murkier and also much more frightening and exciting and joyful than that. Marriage grinds your face into the dirt until you can see new colors and taste new flavors. But you have to show up and invite it all in. You can't hide.

I recently watched *Planet Earth II* with my family, and the footage of various animals waiting not so patiently for their mates to return to the proper rendezvous point in order to make sweet marital bird love or regurgitate a fish smoothie into their throats was enough to send a chill down my spine. *This penguin dad is seriously inept at scaling wave-tossed rocks and at locating his lady in a million-strong crowd of other penguin ladies screeching at the moon together,* I found myself thinking. *Does her screeching have the faintest hint of contempt to it, or am I just imagining that?* Later, as a seabird's baby mama took her time showing up at their appointed meeting spot, I nervously wondered if she'd wandered off with a more dashing seabird and left her devoted mate in the dust. (Okay, he did have a bad habit of pecking in a faintly insecure, unattractive way.) You could see the enormous misunderstandings in play: "You do know that I almost got pulverized against the rocks diving for these fish?" the harried penguin seemed to say with his beady black eyes once he finally arrived.

My younger daughter often proclaims that she will never get married. And why should she want to? As much as I prefer to believe that her father and I are setting a shining example of affectionate, radically open communication, the reality is that she's had a lifelong all-access pass to our version of a penguin marriage: the laborious diplomacy of marital negotiations, the low-key squabbling, the mutual suspensions of disbelief, the subtle undermining, the ever-increasing codependence. After fifteen years of this graceless ballet, it's not surprising that all my daughter wants when she grows up is a tiny house, a subcompact car, and a mini Australian shepherd.

And honestly, there are days when the prospect of growing old next to a mini Aussie doesn't sound so bad when compared to the slowly blossoming garden of horrors inherent to aging in sync with another human. My incredibly handsome and charming husband, who is a tenured professor and looks a solid ten years younger than his numerical age, also has a quick temper, zero depth perception, and a palsy that makes his right hand shake whenever he passes me, say, a porcelain creamer filled to the brim with liquid nitrogen. Even though he and I might've engaged in countless frank and illuminative discussions of our flaws, even though we might've laughed several times about both his palsy and the remarkable ability of liquid nitrogen to cause a searing burn when it comes into contact with living tissue, that doesn't make the ensuing spillage and pain any less real. To be married is to have the words "This is all your fault" eternally poised on the tip of your tongue.

Marriage can feel like a moral litmus test that way. Your challenge is to maintain your composure as the staggering deficits of the highly ineffectual human by your side come into sharper and sharper focus. Somehow you have to keep your sense of humor (which studies suggest is crucial to a healthy marriage), minimize your contempt (a major predictor of marital dissatisfaction), and increase your joint take-home pay (currently the most accurate predictor of how long a marriage will last, according to some studies). So maybe my daughter is onto something. In an upgradable, consumer-driven, instant-gratification world where the experiences of shopping for high-end cell phones, high-end mates, and high-end sperm cells are hauntingly similar to each other, isn't it reasonable to question the value of a legal contract, written in ink, on paper, that involves disastrously punitive terms of dissolution? What kind of an old-fashioned mutant could crave such a primitive trap, particularly when it's paired with an enormously expensive ceremony that often includes allusions to obedience and lifelong mutual suffering and death, of all things? And why do we arbitrarily marry one person instead of, say, two or three or fifteen? Doesn't that place an inordinate amount of pressure on one very fragile penguin?

These days, there are limited economic advantages to marriage, a planet's worth of mates more easily perused and accessed now than ever before in human history, and a host of inconveniences to being married, along with untold drudgery, monotony, frustration, and regret. Add to that the fact that 40 to 50 percent of all marriages in the United States end in divorce anyway. Considering all of that, what could possibly be the point of this outdated charade?

This book represents my personal attempt to understand why I signed myself up for the world's most impossible endurance challenge. Having someone by your side every minute of your life sounds so romantic before he's actually there, making noises, emitting smells, undoing what you've just done, interrupting, undercutting, begging to differ. Sure, I love my husband. But I am still a simple animal, and sometimes I lose the thread. That's when I find myself asking awkward questions, such as: Why do I need a husband, again? And if I'm going to have a husband, shouldn't I have chosen a sturdier one, or maybe one with a fully functioning frontal lobe? Also, why do I get *only one husband*? Wouldn't it be nicer to have a room full of husbands—some creative, others practical, some extremely pretty, others incredibly dexterous?

For years, I figured I was just the sort of weak bird who would rather wait for her very flawed mate to come home than go out preening and showboating just to wind up with another flawed mate in the end. As a married friend of mine said, years ago, when

I asked her if she was tempted to actually *pursue* her younger crush, "No way. He's just another man who'll end up snoring in the bed at night, like all the rest."

But I have to admit, there's something reassuring, to me, about breaking down, falling into disrepair, losing your charms, and misplacing your keys, when you have an equally inept and irritating human tolerating it all, in spite of a million and one very good reasons to put on his walking boots and take his love to town. In other words, if marriage is irrational, as with child-rearing and ambition and art, that's also part of its appeal. Even when my husband and I go through a rough time, bickering more than usual over how many tantrums a twelve-year-old should throw per day or how long a particularly fussy loaf of bread should be left to rise, after we've spent a few weeks staring at our phones at night instead of enjoying each other's company, I can always trust that we'll find each other again. The other day, in the wake of such a market correction, we began our morning walk with the dogs (who are too neurotic to be walked by one person alone), and my husband announced, "When I woke up this morning, the first thing I heard was a voice in my head, telling me, 'You don't have what it takes. You never did and you never will.' " This made us both laugh loudly for a solid block.

Marriage can't always be about living your best lives in sync. Because some of the peak moments of a marriage are when you share in your insecurities, your anxieties, your fears, and your longing. That commitment, the one that can withstand and even revel in the darkest corridors of a life, grows and evolves and eventually transcends a contract or a ceremony the way an ocean overflows and subsumes a thimble of water.

And eventually, as grateful as you are for that bond, sometimes you might wish you didn't recognize its strength. Because some days, it sounds much more fun to feel *less* permanently chained to your spouse. It sounds much more exciting to lose sight of everything, take it all for granted, and make a giant mess of your life instead. Not only would that be far less boring, but also, it could involve world travel, fancy hotels, and male strangers who may or may not own nose-hair-removal devices, but at the very least you've never witnessed them in action.

This book started as an attempt to stop and take a breath after fifteen years of frenetically raising kids alongside my spouse, often without understanding where I was, where we were together, and how we'd grown or regressed along the way. But the more I examined my own marriage, evaluating it and questioning the value of marriage at large, the more I found myself developing an appetite for adventure and novelty. There wasn't anything wrong, exactly. In fact, everything felt *more than* right. It was just that, over the course of my marriage—in part, due to my marriage—I'd transformed from an insecure, flinty young writer into an emotionally secure but existentially ravenous beast. I went from feeling needy and powerless to feeling fully alive and craving even more life. Even though there wasn't a big marital problem to solve, I *created* a series of extra-large problems just by setting out to write a thorough history of my relationship, analyzing it through the good times and the bad. After months of doing this, the marriage almost started to seem like an abstract, *imaginary* thing. And . . . as long as it's imaginary, I might as well destroy it, right? Mmm, yes, doesn't that sound like good, sporting fun?

Even if you still love your spouse very much, just recognizing that he'll be with you until one of you dies is enough to invite your mortality into the room permanently. Over time, marriage itself starts to feel like a slowly unfolding apocalypse. Your marriage will die or you will die. Which ending seems happier?

And then, just as I was finishing the book, death dropped in to say hello. But let's not spoil the best part. All you need to know is that things got very dark, and somewhere along the way, I got lost, but instead of trying to find my way home immediately, I boarded a tiny boat and drifted out to sea, all by myself. Maybe I just wanted to see what dry land looked like from a great distance.

From a distance, the solid ground of marriage has a way of looking mundane and exotic at the same time. My husband Bill is a good person who makes great bread and has a perfect golf swing (not that I know or even care what that means). He also wears golf shirts, which are perhaps the least attractive article of clothing available to humankind. I myself am a wise guru type of writer who knows everything about everything, which makes me about as appealing a mate as Jabba the Hutt, if Jabba talked to his dogs more than his children and blamed his hormones every time he fed someone new to the rancor. We are both catastrophically flawed. But by unearthing our most discouraged moments together without turning away, by screeching at the moon side by side, admitting "This is all our fault," we reaffirm our love and also our intention to face the unknown together, from this point forward.

Sometimes that passion and that resolve feel like they should be measured in the moment, like a firework exploding in the dark sky that says, *Here we are, we're doing this, we intend to stay here as long as we humanly can.*

Will it last until we die? Only a fool would pretend to know the future. Because, as I learned this year, the future is fickle and merciless and she will bend you to her will and change your mind and change it back and then rearrange every cell in your body, just for kicks, until your penguin feels more like a vulture, until your love feels more like hatred, until your prison cell feels more like the only home you'll ever need. Somehow, the whole grueling process starts to feel exhilarating once you welcome everything in. But you have to welcome everything to feel grateful for what you have. You have to stop trying to predict what comes next, and just enjoy the fireworks instead.

2

You Will Be Deeply Loved

Love is madness. Until you fall in love, everything makes sense. Your brain chooses what matters. Your brain is a thoughtful shopper, a detail-oriented assistant. It sorts things into clean piles. Maintains control. Prioritizes. Consolidates your desires. Casts off the impractical, the inconvenient, the unwieldy. Focuses on what's important. Sets limits. Builds walls that don't look too foreboding from the outside. Sews clever disguises. Seals you into a body bag with a clown face on the front.

But inside your body bag, your cells aren't running algorithms. Your cells crave love.

True love: romantic, stupid, blind, sloppy, scary love. Full-body communion, the kind you would raise your sword and fight for. Someone to throw your body across the railroad tracks for. That's not longing, that's satisfaction: Kneeling until your knees hurt. Tracing one red blip on a radar. Crawling into a box under the bed. Swimming to the bottom of the ocean and staying there. Seeking holy communion with another community of cells, a merging of microbiomes, some cells like to call it temporary, other cells like to say it's permanent, gangs form, murderous fandoms, warring tribes, hot blood and splintering bones. That's glory. Learning by bleeding, feeling through osmosis, swimming toward your infinity, sucking on divinity, only right now and also forever.

Your cells decide.

Lust shouts into a bullhorn. Only, try not to take it so personally. Also, please try to take it more personally. You've ignored your cells for too long, and now they're taking the bull by the horns.

Your cells have waited so long for true, blind, sloppy, scary. Don't kill the messenger before you die. Instead, feel the satisfaction of bent knees, a box under the bed, the bottom of the ocean, a patient garden, a hungry nightmare. Your brittle bones still want you to wake up, to snap out of the stupor of logic, to throw out your file cabinets and breathe.

Your cells believe in survival. That's their faith, their church. Your selfish, dirty cells just want to survive. And they want you to have a good time doing it.

My husband and I didn't meet in a little café in Thailand as a storm kicked up outside. We didn't share a compartment on a train to Saint Petersburg in the dead of winter and wind up telling each other our life stories over steaming pots of black tea. We didn't meet on the deck of the USS *Arizona* as it was sinking into shark-filled waters. It wasn't pouring down rain the day that my husband didn't run to my farmhouse in the country and didn't grab my face and didn't declare that he would love me forever.

Bill wrote me an email out of the blue. He told me he had read my writing for years, and he read on my blog that I was newly single. This made him swoon, he wrote. He actually used the word *swoon*—a red flag, in retrospect. A rational, healthy woman would've ignored him, or told him to get lost.

I was neither rational nor healthy at the time. I wrote back immediately: "Send me a picture of your pretty face. But don't expect to be hot enough for me. That doesn't mean I myself am hot. I am just extremely picky."

Bill sent me a photo of his pretty face. "Hubba hubba!" I wrote back.

So many red flags. A universe of red flags. Two matching microbiomes, each composed entirely of red flags. Only lustful cells could make this happen.

This way lies salvation.

$$\infty$$

We sent photos back and forth. "Wow!" he wrote back. "Meow," I wrote. "Whoa," he replied. This went on for a day or two. "Oh my." "Whew!" "Hoo doggie." Along with the pictures, there was clever banter, a mutual puppet show, a shared fantasy that this might mean something. Salvation loomed, quickening the pulse. Immediate investment, immediate surrender. Slowly, we started to exchange other tidbits of information, like the fact that Bill was recently separated and had an eight-year-old son. Lust had no interest in these facts. Yet no divestment followed. Bill sent me a photo of his son, Zeke, but warned me I wouldn't be meeting him for a while. As if I'd been begging for months now to meet his child that I didn't even know existed! Men always act like you're the only one who's overinvested. You can be speeding down the freeway together in the same race car, screaming "Faster, faster!" at the top of your lungs in unison, but they're the ones who suddenly say "Whoa, now, I didn't sign up for this!"

Luckily, I knew better. *This microbiome wants me bad already,* I thought. I sent back a photo of myself with my dog Potus, along with the words "Don't assume that you'll be meeting my little yellow princess anytime soon, because things will have to be *pretty serious* before that happens."

"Sorry for being presumptuous," Bill replied.

But all of this was the fine print. We were already sold. There was no shared train compartment, no pouring rain, no circling sharks. All we needed was a handful of photographs and some witty retorts to get our hopes up way too high. I didn't carefully reflect on the fact that Bill was separated but not yet divorced and had a son. Bill didn't thoughtfully analyze the fact that I was already bossy and moody and very demanding over email. I even wrote "I'm bossy and moody and very demanding" in one of my emails.

"You're a woman, in other words," Bill replied. This didn't strike me as sexist so much as pragmatic, possibly because I was *also* sexist. And pragmatic. I was thirty-four years old. Bill was forty-one. We were both old enough to know a few things. We were also old enough to know better.

We matched. It was obvious. Here was a man who could string together words in all the right ways. I ate his words. His words made me feel things. He was honest and cynical and apologetic and vulnerable and guarded. He read my words and encouraged me to send more words. He didn't even seem to mind long-winded digressions. I didn't know yet how important that was. He insulted himself. He said he liked to drink and he also liked to surf. He was a thoughtful professor who was also into simpleminded leisure. I owned a house and a dog and had a solid job and a good sense of humor and I was also intense and eloquent and afraid, very afraid.

Lust forms a tidal wave. Lust picks you up and hurls you into the sky, far above the racing ocean. You are about to be ground into the sand, but it feels like deliverance.

∞

One day, right after we exchanged emails, I was looking for something in my overstuffed purse but I was only coming up with old pennies and dog hair and tufts of lint, and I started to panic about how cool I was trying to seem to Bill. I imagined this tall, handsome professional, taking one look at my dog-hair-covered house and my dumb clothes and realizing that I wasn't even close to his caliber of human. I was just a growly little nerd playing a dream girl on the internet. He would immediately recognize that all of his time spent crafting clever emails had been wasted.

As I had this thought, I pulled a tiny slip of paper out of my purse. It was a crumpled fortune from a cookie. I unfolded and read it:

You will be deeply loved.

∞

I wanted a husband from a very young age. If that sounds regressive, that's because it is. But really, what good is a boyfriend? A boyfriend is, by definition, impermanent. He is temporary filler, a disposable prop, a transitional object, a traveling salesman. Why invest time and energy into someone who'll disappear in a year or two? Disappearing is baked into the boyfriend picture. If he didn't disappear, he'd be a husband. Who wants to shove all of your beauty and youth and light straight into a boyfriend-shaped garbage bag, when you know you'll eventually drag it out to the curb, and someone will come to take it to the dump in the morning?

I spent close to two decades looking for a husband. I didn't just want someone who could temporarily soothe my loneliness. I wanted someone who would banish loneliness and darkness forever. I didn't want a role player. I wanted a franchise player, someone to build my whole program around.

I wanted a *husband*. One that looked nice.

By the age of thirty-four, I wanted a husband that matched my other stuff: my scrappy house, my badly behaved dog, my full-time job. I wanted a *grown adult* husband. I'd had enough of these half-baked (in more ways than one) man-children. I wanted more. I wanted a partner with a solid career to match my own. I wanted a hunky, square-jawed, mature listener.

But that wasn't all. I also wanted a nurturing daddy type who would hang on my every word. And I wanted an athlete. (Why not hold out for an athlete? *What, you don't think I deserved one?*)

I wanted an intellectual who was also a comedian, but with a nice ass. I wanted a cross between a therapist and a cowboy. Those existed somewhere, probably! And if they existed, *I* deserved to have one. I was done settling for these wilty, noncommittal, barely employed *baby* boyfriends. I wanted a swaggery, self-assured *husband* man. I deserved a permanent, talented franchise player, damn it!

After about two weeks of exchanging emails, I was pretty sure that Bill could support a whole franchise. He was a grown adult. He was an intellectual comedian, an athletic therapist. He had talent. He had potential. He needed a little guidance, but I trusted my coaching skills. I could build a solid program around this one.

But all husbands, like all franchise players, have their flaws. They are only human. That is, in fact, the real tragedy of finding a permanent husband: He is a husband, yes, but he is not omnipotent. He is not a demigod. He does not have golden sunlight and magic shooting out of his fingertips. He cannot banish darkness and bend the laws of time and space. This is a recurring letdown for those of us who succeed in locating an actual adult human husband. Even with skilled coaching, Kobe had his issues. Shaq had his little flaws—which, on some days, from the wrong angle, might just look like very big flaws. Fatal flaws, even.

That said, my coaching has its flaws too. I could give even the most confident player a complex. I have tremendously high expectations. I push my players too hard. Everyone says so.

I *believed* in him, though. Or maybe I didn't. Maybe that was the problem. *But goddamn it, do we want to be champions or don't we?*

∞

Bill had read my cartoons. He had read my TV column. He had even read my blog, which was rambling and aggressive. He was a true fan. But did he have any *talent*? This is what Jerry West might ask about, say, Rick Fox. *Yes, we know you love the Lakers. That's all very well and good. But do you really have what it takes to be a Laker? We're not so sure of that.*

Bill was definitely handsome: thick brown hair, big brown eyes, square jaw, dimples. He was gainfully employed, and he happened to be a big fan of the program I was running. This was my Shaq.

I didn't know it yet, but he was also my Kobe: cocky, intractable. Taking the same shot over and over, even when it's not working. He was a bad learner who thought he was a good learner (somewhat ironic, for a professor of education). Lunkheaded and goofy and fun like Shaq, but thin-skinned and defensive and imperious like Kobe. *Yeah, we get it, you speak Italian. You still have to work on your jump shot in the paint, buddy. Yes, you're very pretty, but your shooting percentage is abysmal for huge stretches of the game. You know that, right?*

I had two franchise players wrapped into one, and I didn't even know it.

I was still worried that he might not be ready. So right before we met, I wrote him an email warning him that I ran a pretty tight program and he might be pushed to the limits of his abilities for the first time. People always assume that love is all about celebrating someone else's amazing qualities, I wrote. But true love is also about accepting another person's flaws. In order to create a love that grew and adapted over the years, you had to commit to someone else's flaws the same way you commit to their qualities. That was love. Loving someone's bouts of neediness and self-loathing the way you love their hot face.

Was I writing this email to Bill, or to myself? And was it remotely sane to write the word "commitment" before you meet someone in person?

Bill probably should've replied, "Why don't you just relax? We haven't even met yet." But he didn't. That would be like Shaq telling Jerry West he didn't really care if he wound up playing for the Lakers or the Timberwolves, because any team would do. That would be like Kobe telling Phil Jackson he could just as easily play for Jeff Van Gundy.

I was betting that my franchise talent would come through. And he did. He wrote: "Your words moved me." This is as close to being passionately kissed in the rain as it gets, at least for a writer. Sitting at my desk on an overcast October afternoon, I felt absolutely giddy. *I moved him deeply.* Nothing feels better than trying to reach someone, using only your ideas and feelings and beliefs, and *actually succeeding.* It's hard to do that when you're face to face, thinking about whether or not your lips are chapped. I felt like we were building something together already, something breathtaking and sublime, a reason for all of our cells to stand at attention, to sing in fifty-billion-part harmony together, to crave more and more and more.

But I don't want to belabor this part of my story. Because the truth is that being in love looks the same no matter who's doing it. Watching someone fall in love is like watching someone eat a really big, sloppy submarine sandwich. The more they're enjoying their sandwich, the less enjoyable it is to watch them eat it. Savor your true love as much as you can, just have the good grace to do so in private.

When I met Bill, I was a grown adult. I had projects. I had friends. I threw parties. I walked my dog. I paid my bills. I exercised. I weeded my yard.

But I was still a giant baby. I wanted a man who magically filled in all of the gaps in my life. I wanted a man who would move neatly into my world and do whatever I wanted, whenever I wanted it. I wanted a flexible sidekick. I wanted a daddy. I wanted a best friend. I wanted a masseuse. I wanted a drinking buddy. I wanted a housekeeper. I wanted a life coach. I wanted a boss. I wanted a handservant.

I wanted way too much, and I wasn't that realistic about what I'd actually get. But when I met Bill for the first time, it was easy to believe that he'd simply *be* everything I wanted, forever. He stood on my front doorstep, tall and slightly nerdy, smiling his nervous smile, shifting his weight in his bad shoes, and I was not disappointed. I could immediately tell that we were going to have a lot to talk about, that we were going to have a great time, that this night was going to be one I remembered for a long time. I stood there, feeling pretty in my favorite cords and shitkicker boots, feeling young and shiny and funny and smart, and I knew for a fact that he was going to love me like crazy, maybe a little more than he wanted to. That was a refreshing feeling, in the wake of watching my most recent stoner boyfriend carry his life-size cutout replica of the Emperor from *Star Wars* out my front door with the rest of his things. It was good to feel like a man was old enough and wise enough to see me clearly for a change, and to want what he saw.

So Bill came in and met my dog Potus and then we got into his filthy Ford Escort station wagon (this guy was still a fixer-upper for sure) and drove to an Italian restaurant around the block.

The wait list for the restaurant was so long that we went to the bar next door instead. We drank pints of Guinness and talked excitedly and then a little drunkenly for hours. It was fun and easy.

And then about two hours into it, Bill said something about how he was newly separated. Even though his marriage had been dead for years and even though he'd dated a bunch of women over the past eight months since he finally moved out from living with his ex-wife, he still couldn't get into anything serious any time soon.

"No worries, I am also juggling a few different boyfriends at once, honestly," I told him with the casualness of a defense coach staring at a clipboard and only half-listening. "Although I do have one opening thanks to a recent departure. You can be boyfriend number five." I know you're thinking there's no way that I was that smooth, but you're wrong. I was so goddamn smooth. Ask Phil Jackson, he'll tell you. When you know you're recruiting the guy, it's like you get into the zone. You're *not* going to fuck it up, no matter what.

Bill looked relieved that I was so unflappable about his supposed need for time and space. And even though I really *was* trying to avoid jumping into a relationship before I knew who I was dealing with, I got a little scared at how relieved he looked.

"I'll be right back!" I announced, a very nerdy habit of mine when going to the bathroom, because what? I'm not coming back? I ducked into a bathroom stall and sat down and covered my eyes with my hands and said to myself, "No fucking way this is happening all over again." I was scared out of my head. Because I was already too invested, and I knew it. And with straight men, you truly never knew. They could spend weeks trying to get into your pants, with the full knowledge that there was no damn way they were signing on to a lifetime with your bossy ass. And even though I'd done my own share of eating samples without making a purchase, this time I wanted more, much more.

So I calmed down and got back into the zone. I said to myself, "Don't fuck this up. Do not go out there and ask him to specify *exactly* what he means by 'not serious' and 'not ready.' Do not demand a timeline and a mission statement. Do not even occupy a space where you are *curious* about these things. You go back out there and you drink your goddamn beer and you shut the fuck up about what comes next." I mean, imagine Phil Jackson getting insecure and sending Michael Jordan a bullet-pointed email about whether or not he's truly ready to pick up and move to Chicago. No! Let's get practical, here!

I returned to the table with jokes about boyfriend number five on the tip of my tongue. And soon after that we returned to my house and we kissed and it felt exactly right, better than right, and I even sent him home without having sex with him first. I was not myself, in other words. I was behaving with dignity and self-respect for a change.

I believed that this love would stay, and I wouldn't have to work hard at it—it would be *easy* this time. I believed that we would be happy forever and ever. I believed that this man would never give up on me. That was the one thing I was right about. I was wrong about everything else.

What's so interesting about falling in love? Our culture tends to zoom in on those first locked eyes, that first passionate kiss, and then fade out just as things are starting to get interesting. I say skip over that stuff and show me your first conversation about recurring minor digestive issues, your first long car trip across unremarkable terrain, your first encounter with each other's least emotionally stable relative. I want every romantic comedy to open on a couple's first detailed discussion of past dental work, and I want it to end with a two-hour-long game of Monopoly, in which our dashing hero is forced to mortgage Boardwalk, then he has a spectacular meltdown and quits the game in a blizzard of fake money and flying red plastic hotels.

When I was twenty-seven years old, I had just moved to Los Angeles and I was fixated on falling in love. So I set out to write *the most romantic* romantic comedy ever. Then I found out what a rom-com really was: either you show two people wanting each other more and more while fate keeps them apart, or you show two people *hating* each other more and more, but then realizing that their hatred is actually love. Two people can't just fall in love and stay that way. Then there's no story. We need suspense and tension and unresolved problems and the faintest suspicion that what they really want is to destroy each other.

In other words, cinematically what we want is a long marriage. We want to see things unravel before they even begin. We want a clear preview of the misery to come.

Whether we know it consciously or only sense it subconsciously, we have some shared, murky awareness that hatred and love are the same thing: you love what you `hate, and hate what you love. Your hatred has power because it points back to your weaknesses. Your hatred makes you feel small and helpless. Your hatred gives you a motive, an attraction, a reason to try. Your hatred fuels you. Your hatred turns you on, in other words. You have to bring every tool and every strength at your disposal when you do battle against something you hate. See how we're talking about sex now?

Nothing is hotter than hating someone and then joining forces with them, or trying to join them and failing. Envy is in the mix, too. When you're attracted to someone, nine times out of ten you simply want what that person has. Or you want to *be* that person. Or you think they don't deserve what they have, so you want to steal it from them and maybe destroy them in the process.

Most divorces aren't some unfortunate, unforeseen accident. They're the natural manifestation of a couple's destiny together: *This is the tragic dance we've been called to perform over the course of one or two decades.* But which is the better act of revenge: Divorcing, or staying married and slowly driving your spouse mad over the course of thirty to seventy years?

Even though every romantic comedy ever written lays this basic equation out for us, we tend to miss the essential conflict that lies at the heart of passionate love. Those moments you realize you might hate someone forever are an echo of the moments you realize that you might love someone forever. The forever part speaks to the fever inside you, a feeling strong enough that it's impossible to imagine it lifting. When you're very sick, you imagine that you'll never be well again. When you're very sick of someone, you imagine that they will torture you until your dying days. When you're in love with someone, you imagine that they might make you happy forever. When you have great chemistry with someone, you imagine that you're both omnipotent, like some powerful force is being channeled through you. Together, you are a tree being struck by lightning. You are an island in a Category 5 hurricane.

This is why romance novels, with their endless amorous gestures and passionate kisses, feel like watching someone do an interpretive dance about a cathedral they once visited. If you try to describe love directly, it sounds too mundane. If you describe sex in concrete terms, it feels too clinical. When romance novels offer up the concrete details of sex, it feels about as tangential as describing the toppings on the best pizza you ever ate. Heaving breasts, a ripped corset, panting, sweating: extra cheese, onions, mushrooms, lots of sausage. Even if it's the best pizza you've ever met, how are you going to make that clear using concrete, secular words, after the fact, without making someone imagine any old pizza in the known universe? Forget the mechanics of the moment. The bottom line is, you got struck by lightning. It doesn't matter how it happened, all that matters is that now you're dizzy and your hair is on fire.

I want to smell the smoke, and see you try to walk forward without falling down. Let's gloss over the heavy petting and dive straight into the good stuff: Our heroine hears her true love repeat the same story he's already told her three times before. Her eyes register disbelief: *How is this happening?*

It's hard not to question his judgment, once this flaw emerges. But then it just keeps reemerging. She wants to put an end to it, once and for all! But now there are children in the room, so she needs to censor herself. She bites her tongue, then spots a sippy cup that needs to be set upright, then notices that his wineglass is dripping a stain onto their coffee table, because this man refuses to acknowledge the existence of coasters. That's where the lightning goes, eventually: into her flushed face, when she surveys his latest art installation, Burgundy Circles in Wood. She rushes off to find a rag. She is turning into her mother.

"What does it mean to become your mother?" turns out to be a central question of marriage, along with countless other big, uncomfortable questions, most of them spawned by something as small as a ring of red wine. A long drive across the plains of Texas incites an existential morass: How do you drag an intractable beast and your matching mini-beasts in the direction of what you think might be the Most Important Experiences? A game of Scrabble yields to questions of dominance and submission. An afternoon of weeding the garden ends in an argument about toxic plants. A simple inquiry—"What are we going to do about dinner?"— incites an existential crisis, the 742nd of its kind since your wedding day.

When something small that this person does, this person you love and hate with equal passion, pushes you into a black pit of despair, questioning yourself and the world and everyone in it, the dimensions of your perception shift, the landscape stretches out, bleak and confusing, the sky bends and warps the light of the sun. How do you escape this hallucination of too much feeling? Is this an illusion, or is it the tide of emotions that live just beneath the surface of your skin at all times? What fantasies might protect you from these terrors? Which distractions might numb you into tolerating these eternally locked horns?

Why is this person always the same, and always in the way—a mumbling roadblock, a pointy Lego brick underfoot, a smelly heap of laundry blocking the bathroom door—and also, somehow, the only path back to sanity? How do you push aside your hatred and dig for your love, when it feels easier and more fun to just write the guy off forever, move your stuff into a big van, pack up the dogs and the crying kids, leave this sad specimen alone in the dust of a life you've clearly outgrown? Maybe the next one will be less defensive when he's mad.

And yet. The sad man alone on the porch breaks your heart, in spite of your firm intentions to get gone forever. The dummy who doesn't use coasters? He matters. When you play Monopoly, he's always the dog and never the cowboy. You are the cowboy, as it turns out. He always buys Boardwalk, even though no one ever lands on it, because he's bad at learning. This is the one man you enjoy crushing the most. This is also the man you enjoy saving the most. You *are* your mother. Maybe that's okay. Maybe that's the whole point.

Being married is far more interesting than falling in love. The gritted teeth. The clenched jaw. Agony in a half-open, half-empty cereal box. Longing in a badly washed dish. Slow evolution, or a slow unraveling: It can be hard to tell which. It all boils down to faith, the ability to trust the fates, to accept your role as the cowboy, to love your dog, even though he's horribly trained. You need to be prepared to watch your franchise player miss 80 percent of his shots in a game. Because marriages survive on a wave of forgiveness. And marriages die when you can't forgive yourself.

Or maybe your spouse truly *is* terrible. I mean, that's always a possibility. But when your spouse is mostly good, or *almost* good enough, and you're sometimes not so good at all, then you have to forgive yourself. It's not easy. That's what makes it so interesting.

∞

Marriage is a lifelong market correction to true love's overvaluation. Marriage is reaping what you sow. Marriage is paying the piper. But somehow it feels good, to get your comeuppance, to take your punishment. Why does it feel so good to realize you're wrong, over and over again? Maybe that's what separates people whose marriages stick together from people whose marriages die: a little masochism and a lifelong love of learning (whether they're actually good learners or not).

Even so, I don't want to watch two people falling in love and then turning themselves into masochists. Being married for years makes you a tiny bit allergic to witnessing love in others, but you're also hopelessly romantic under your layers of suspicion and cynicism. Marriage turns you into a strange mix of optimist and pessimist. You can't relate to the falling in love, madly and deeply—it looks so gross from here!—but then suddenly, you're smiling and sighing in spite of yourself. You can't bear the foolishness of watching two people sign on to a lifetime together, and the next thing you know you're weeping.

My default mode on most busy days is withdrawn cynicism. But then, suddenly, I'm standing next to the washing machine and I take in my husband, in his soft pants, looking for a screwdriver. My cells soak in the breathtaking architecture of his bones. I reach for him and he never backs away when I do that—never. I kiss him with feeling, and it's like all of my nagging questions about what the fuck is wrong with me melt into a warm certainty that I am good and he is good and good choices brought us here, to this hallway. Marriages are best celebrated in hallways, when there's no time: he's about to leave and I want more than what I'm getting from the day so far. I want to relish this man.

Nevertheless, it's still hard to remember falling in love with Bill. Acrobatic images come to mind, but I'm going to take your delicate sensibilities into account and not describe them in detail here. Mostly what I picture is a rumpled bed, covered in an assortment of aged cheeses and cured meats, and a bottle of wine, some of it spilled. I imagine us laughing and eating and other naked things that won't sound interesting to you, but it was the best pizza I ever ate in my life. Then someone is explaining how they were in high school. Then someone describes their first job. Then someone is chuckling over what an asshole this one ex-boyfriend was. The stakes are low. The difficulty level is beginner.

Now you think I'm not a romantic, but you're wrong. I'm romantic about the long story. I'm not romantic about building your little delusional house on the prairie. I'm romantic about trying desperately to repair the walls of your house by the banks of Plum Creek, as they start to crumble unexpectedly. I want to see you figure out how to play hearts with your spouse without throwing your drink in his face. I want to see you hand over the baby and then resist the urge to immediately tell him that he's doing it wrong. I want to watch you lose your doughnuts over something as stupid as how your husband navigates using a map. I want to see you seethe for a solid hour, and then figure out that *you're* the one who messed up the most, *you're* the one with the out-of-control temper, *you're* the one who needs to calm the fuck down. I want to witness how you speak to each other right after you discover that the car's completely out of oil, or the roof is leaking, or his cousin, who's staying upstairs, might not leave until next month.

Falling in love is scary, but it's not confusing. When you're in love, you know you have to go for it, no matter what. It's like standing outside an abandoned house you've heard is haunted. The giant wooden door beckons you. You knock, but no one answers. You try the handle—it's open! You've got a chill down your spine. You feel so alive! This is the moment you've been waiting for!

We all know you'll go into the house. We can skip that part. We all know you'll push open that heavy door and you'll walk into the front hallway and it will be even darker and more frightening than you imagined. You'll be scared, but you'll also feel brave. You'll be excited and turned on and giddy with fear.

And then the door will slam shut behind you, and the dead bolt will thump into place. *Now* we're cooking with gas. Now you'll learn some things: about your deepest insecurities, your buried desires, your weaknesses. Now you'll grow up. *Or else.*

When I fell in love with Bill, there was so much I didn't know. I didn't know we would feel so much. I didn't know it would be so terrifying.

$$\infty$$

One afternoon in the first few months we were dating, Bill and I took my dog Potus, who was nine months old at the time, to a burrito place in Venice. We sat outside in the sunshine to eat our lunch. Potus had a cast on her front paw because she'd broken her toe.

A pit bull was walking without a leash, without an owner, across the street. The dog spotted Potus and crossed the street. That was before I knew that Potus was an extremely dominant dog, and even with a cast up to her elbow, she would throw an imperious glance at any dog alive, even if it meant that violence would soon follow. Potus longed for the stab of eviscerating jaws. That was just a core trait, maybe genetic. She wanted to die in battle if possible. She didn't mind, if she could taste hot blood before the lights went out.

The dogs went for each other's throats, but mostly what we and the people around us saw was a pit bull attacking a puppy. I screamed but I couldn't move. I may have tugged ineffectually on Potus's leash to get her away from the dog. Bill stood up and grabbed the pit bull by the scruff of its neck and tossed it back across the sidewalk. The pit bull stopped and started walking back toward us, more slowly this time. Potus was barking and straining at her leash—MORE BLOOD PLEASE—but Bill stepped in front of her. A guy at a nearby table who was right next to the pit bull grabbed it by the collar.

I was whimpering and holding Potus back. Bill spoke calmly to the guy holding the pit bull. Someone said they'd seen the dog before, maybe they could take the dog somewhere and ask about something. Bill thanked everyone and then asked if I was okay and checked Potus's ears for puncture wounds.

This was before I knew that Bill could navigate certain types of emergencies without panicking or making an even bigger scene. Even though he became frazzled and reactive over all kinds of small things, this was the sort of crisis he could handle. He was diplomatic and efficient.

I could deal with different kinds of crises. But that day, as Bill was kneeling over Potus to make sure she wasn't badly hurt, I didn't notice that he was wearing ugly pants or that his sideburns didn't do his pretty face justice. That day, I saw the truth: This was a grown adult man who knew what he was doing. And I had never dated someone like that before. I was a tree struck by his lightning.

Eventually, stress and conflict would warp our perception of each other. We couldn't dodge the high stakes of signing up to each other until death. We would try to find fantasies to hide us from these terrors. We would look for distractions to numb us, to protect us from each other. But that day, we were an island in a hurricane. *This is how it should feel,* I thought. *This is what I've been looking for.*

Love is glorious and electric. I can feel it all now, at last. I remember. There's nothing else that comes close to touching that full-body communion, the kind you would raise your sword and fight for. You'll do whatever it takes to have everything, right now and also forever. There is nothing better.

3

True Romance

Romance is an act of imagination, fueled by fear. My perfect future husband and I don't know that yet, as we begin planning our first trip to Europe, scrutinizing blurry photos of hotel rooms in Le Marais and San Sebastián to discern if they're the suitable mix of sophisticated and scrappy, skimming menus and considering attractions, packing ordinary clothes for these extraordinary places. We have faith that we will become extraordinary on the beaches at Biarritz. We are certain that, in the gorgeous corridors of Barcelona, his eyes will sparkle, my hair will form a luxurious, fluffy frame around my face. We're sure that romance will elevate us to a higher level of consciousness and gorgeousness and confidence. We are in love, after all. We have found our person. This is the start of a whole new life. All former selves—intractable, lumpy, ungrateful, repetitive, needy—will be left behind.

But our former selves disagree. They are packing their bags for their first trip to Europe, too. They know they have the power to ruin everything. Imagine how romantic it will be, to destroy a very good thing—the best one yet, by far! Our former selves snicker behind their hands as they pack. They can't wait.

∞

Some might say the romance of this romantic trip began the morning we left for Paris. As we waited for our cab outside my perfect future husband's apartment, I felt a leaf in my hair and tried to pull it out, only to find a crushed, furry bee between my fingers. Others might argue that, as the plane tilted and rumbled across the Atlantic and my bee sting swelled to the size of a plum, that was when the real romance began. Others would zoom in on that first night in the closet-sized Parisian hotel room with the slanted stairs and slanted floors, the room spinning from what I would later recognize as vertigo, my heart despairing that every corner of Paris does not smell like the pages of glossy lady magazines. They'd say the romance began the second I realized that when you walk the streets of Paris for the very first time, you do not *always* feel like a great glowing god, optimistic and invincible.

In fact, it is possible to feel queasy and ugly and stupid on the streets of Paris. It's possible to find the corner café too crowded and smoky, to encounter the tiny brasseries and flower stands as cartoonish imitations of a France that might've vanished decades ago. It's possible to find the French themselves *a teensy bit too French*. Not only that, but it's possible to reach into one's brain for a single sentence from six years of French in junior high, high school, and college, and discover an utter void. And after fumbling for words and mumbling something in English *like a common tour-*

ist *who has never been to Paris even once,* after the waiter rolls his eyes and theatrically turns on his heel, revealing himself to be a bad imitation of a breed of French waiter that might've died off around the time Hemingway last set foot on the continent, after looking down at an idiotic crepe—we might as well be at Universal Studios Hollywood!—after all of that, I looked to my perfect, handsome, smart, amazing future husband for comfort and reassurance, and saw that he was a little bit . . . unsteady. He was looking back with worried eyes, wondering if, like Paris itself, he was a big letdown. He was so insecure, this man! How had I not noticed that before? And in that exceptionally frightening and thus deeply romantic moment, it was suddenly possible to find my handsome, smart, amazing future husband . . . disappointing.

$$\infty$$

What's more disappointing? The fact that he actually cares what you're feeling, which for some crazy reason makes you angry and self-conscious, or the fact that he doesn't bluster his way through his nonexistent French so much as cringe and cower visibly? This is what all of your former selves are debating in delighted tones as you take the fast train from Paris to Biarritz, your head swimming and your bee sting, now the size of a peach, throbbing. This is not how your arrogant father behaved when he was traveling, your former selves remind you. Your dad dove in and swaggered his way through it all, and you felt safe and secure (if sometimes slightly embarrassed). Your future husband has no swagger. His fears amplify your fears.

But what do you want? your former selves hiss in your ear as the landscape whizzes by and your future husband smiles nervously in your direction. *Do you seriously want a daddy? You're so weak that you can't travel to Europe for the first time without wanting your future husband to imitate your dead father?*

This moment, as the train pulls into Biarritz and your self-hatred starts to upstage your hatred of your future husband, might just be the starting point of the real, true romance. The rain lets up enough for the two of you to find a table by the ocean, and as you sit there, you notice that you are surrounded by a wide range of bored international types with money, families with adult children, all of them with the same triple-processed hair carrying the same Gucci and Hermès bags, all of them trussed up in tight jeans and blousy blouses. You might as well be at the Grove in Los Angeles. You might as well be in Miami or New Jersey or Pleasanton, California.

This is not the *real* France, the real Europe! You arrived a decade too late—maybe two or three decades too late. You could've come as a student and stayed in hostels and gotten drunk on red wine with greasy delicious strangers, but instead you are dragging along with you a disappointing middle-aged dope like an unwieldy, oversized suitcase without wheels. He has nothing to say, you can see that now. He tries to make up for it by reading street signs out loud in a cheerful voice, like some kind of confused half-wit. He is *such* a nerd and he's wearing—is that a golf shirt?

This is where the roller coaster starts climbing the really steep hill that will almost certainly bring your death. At this moment when you recognize for the first time that you are wasting a literal fortune just to lug an extra large man-shaped bag through a long-ago-destroyed, overpriced tourist wasteland, as your pulse races and you realize that this charmless mountain of wincing leather will soon propose marriage to you, of all things, that's when you know in your heart that all lives peter out early and become miserable descents into old age and disappointment. Heterosexual women like yourself only pair up with a man because they know they're going to be miserable anyway, so they might as well have a guy around to carry things and fetch the car and ask for the check.

Why a man, *though?* your former selves whisper as your oversized luggage orders a second lukewarm beer. Why spend the rest of your life with *a man*, of all things? Men, you now see clearly, are tedious beasts with nothing to offer, nothing to add. Why not bring your closest female friends to Europe? There's nothing you'd like better than to have your girlfriends here instead, drinking and snickering with you about the bad waiter. Why do you and your lady friends isolate yourselves into miserable pairs instead? Why not marry your friends? Why not marry a nice dog or a gentle horse? Marrying a man is like ordering an imitation crepe in an imitation of a café in an imitation of Paris. Why marry an inadequate replica? You will merely seal yourself into a wax museum of your own creation.

One might presume that the point when you began to write off all monogamous heterosexual human relations from a few centuries ago to the present *could* mark the apex of the romance in this heady story of romance! One could be forgiven for presuming this. Because as you trudged through the streets of San Sebastián, flanked by soccer—yes, football!—fans pissing on the cobblestone streets, as you boarded an overnight train to Barcelona, your head knocking into the side of the train car for hours, as you finally entered those narrow old streets, sleep-deprived, your jet-lag-induced vertigo kicking up again, you issued a deeply romantic warning to your future husband.

"I know you're probably planning to propose on this trip," you recall yourself saying. "Don't speak, just listen very closely to me. Don't propose when I'm tired and dizzy, like I am today. I'm PMSing right now. Don't propose while I'm still PMSing. Make sure I'm at least showered. And don't buy me some bubble-gum-machine ring. I want a *real* engagement ring. Don't propose until you have a real ring. But I don't want to talk about it."

Your overstuffed bag looked at you, disappointed. *Handle everything*, is what you meant, *with confidence, with swagger*. But do it later. Much, much later.

"Okay. I hear you." That's all he said, because he literally has nothing to say, ever, like all men.

Maybe I was buying myself some time. Maybe I knew by then that our former selves had stowed away on the plane with us, and I didn't want his self-doubting former self proposing to my hormonal, ugly, resentful former self. I didn't want him to ask me to marry him with a question mark in his voice, asking not just "Will you marry me?" but also "Is this a stupid idea?" and "Am I good enough for you?" and "Are you good enough for me, or are you actually completely terrible?"

I wanted him to be sure, because I wasn't. I wasn't sure if I was good enough for him or for myself or for marriage. I wasn't sure I wanted to spend forever with anyone, least of all myself. But I was very, very sure, at that particular moment on our trip, that nothing would ever make me happy. I was utterly unlovable, and that meant I would drag him to hell with me.

I wasn't wrong about that. Because when we arrived at our hotel north of Valencia, we finally broke into a giant fight—about how tedious and repugnant he insisted on being, maybe, or about choosing the wrong hotel or about something even smaller, who knows? (You can fight with an overpacked bag about anything under the sun, trust me.) And I yelled at my perfect future husband. I yelled at him in my bad sleep shorts, with my tangled, ugly hair on my hideous head, and as I yelled I thought, *This will release me from this purgatorial entanglement! I'm free! I am disgusting, and I deserve to be alone forever! Finally, my future husband has stormed out. Success!*

He returned a half hour later. He sat next to me on the bed, where I was reading. He was apologetic, which was helpful, yet also unattractive. Then he spoke. "There was a jewelry festival of some kind downstairs—," and he started to reach into his pocket.

This time I didn't just yell. "NO!" I shrieked. "I told you I didn't want this!" I wailed like someone about to jump off a cruise ship and drown in the salty sea. I screeched like a woman smothering all of her former selves under an avalanche of self-loathing. I howled like a woman murdering the best thing that had ever happened to her, ruining the absolute best relationship with the kindest, most patient, most defensive, most exasperating, most handsome, most hideous man she had ever met. I bellowed and sobbed and snotted into my pillow, in my bad sleep shorts, with my messy hair, and my future husband yelled back, telling me I was terrible, finally admitting that I was awful, awful and unlovable, things I knew all along but wanted to hear out loud, and in English.

My disappointing future husband sat in the bathroom of our disappointing hotel room on a disappointing stretch of Spanish coastline for about twenty minutes. Then he came out. He did not show me the (probably disappointingly bad) ring he'd bought. We talked in ragged tones about what was happening to us. I cried.

He sulked. We talked some more. We cuddled ambivalently on the uncomfortable mattress of the bad bed in the bad room, hating ourselves and each other, hating Spain and Europe and the whole planet and the inky black void beyond it.

$$\infty$$

The next morning we drove down the coast, sunshine streaming into the windows of our tiny rental car, over empty, winding roads. *The south of Spain!* a voice inside my head gushed. We stopped at a place called the Auto Grill. Among the lukewarm pieces of pizza and wilted-looking salads, I found a sandwich made of fresh bread (finally!), manchego, and *jamón ibérico* wrapped in paper. My future husband found some very good olives and another sandwich with other cured meats involved, and we ate our sandwiches in the front seat of our tiny rental car in the parking lot, and we didn't talk much.

All of us were there, our former selves and our current selves. We were excited and melancholy and needy and pissy and impatient and satisfied. And *that* was the most romantic moment of this very romantic story. Because as we sat and chewed, we realized that love had not transformed us into great, glowing gods, optimistic and invincible. Instead, all of our former and current selves would be packed into that tiny car like temperamental clowns, and our agony wouldn't end when our trip was over. We were in for a rough ride that would last a lifetime, or even longer. Maybe we would even be jammed together like sardines in the afterlife. Anything was possible.

We ate our cured meats in silence, and every now and then,

we looked into each other's eyes and we didn't look away quickly. Because we knew that it was possible to be disgusted and annoyed and bored and still feel love—pounding, elated, passionate. In that moment, we were disheveled and ordinary, and also gorgeous and extraordinary. We matched. Nothing is more romantic than being totally in sync, even if that means you're totally doomed. Bill and I were both terrified, but we knew we weren't turning back. We were sure.

4

The Jumpy Castle

One year before I met Bill, I bought a small white house with bright-blue trim in Highland Park, a scrappy neighborhood northeast of Los Angeles. Carlos, my neighbor across the street, told me that he'd always thought the house looked just like a fish restaurant. He brought me a bottle of water when I was walking around my new yard, peering in the windows, while the house was still in escrow. Carlos had a daughter he loved and an ex-wife he hated and parents who were impossible. He lived with his parents and his daughter. His neighbors on the left were crazy, he told me, and they didn't talk to him. His neighbor on the right was also crazy—a composer who lived alone and walked around in his underwear during the summer. One summer afternoon, I saw the composer outside on the sidewalk in his underwear, true to Carlos's prophecy. He was cocking his head at the sound of a truck backing up. He tried to sing along with the backing-up sound. "Eeep eeep eep. Is that a C? Eeep. Maybe C-sharp."

My house was halfway up a steep hill, so my neighbors to the right, a family with three kids in a two-story house, loomed over my lot. My neighbors to the left, three single men in three small houses that shared a large dusty brown lot, were beneath me. I could watch the one guy working on his boat. I could smell the lighter fluid from the other guy's grill, which sat a few feet below my dining room window.

Below me, they enjoyed their solitude: Cold beers at dusk. A little gardening on a quiet afternoon. A little grilling at sunset. Across the street, Carlos was often kneeling in his garden, planting something, watering something, mostly to avoid his parents inside. "My parents," he'd say, and then make a yapping-dog shape with his hand. Next to him, the composer would sometimes stand on the sidewalk with wild hair, soaking in the world around him with visible pleasure. "Do you smell that?" he would ask, gesturing at the oleander bushes in front of his house or maybe the honeysuckle vines up the street. "It smells wonderful out here."

But above me, there was chaos: three chihuahuas, barking and running in tight circles, and three daughters shrieking at each other, with two parents always silent, always hidden. Sometimes the youngest girl, who was three, would come and stand at the fence in her backyard, six feet above me, and stare at me. Occasionally she'd try to talk to me in a baby language I didn't understand. "Dah," she'd say, pointing at the dog. I knew I wanted kids someday. I'd always wanted kids; I'd never wavered on that front. But that didn't mean I actually liked them.

"Yes, dog," I'd answer. "Dah," she'd repeat. It got boring quickly. She'd never walk away, so I'd have to.

Two or three times a year, her parents would rent a jumpy

castle that took up their entire side yard. Because their house was so close, I could hear the kids inside the jumpy castle all day and all night, screeching as they leaped and lurched and stumbled all over each other, as they shrieked and giggled and cried when another kid stepped on one of their heads or one of the smaller ones rolled right out onto the pavement, like a baby sliding out of a giant, shaking purple womb.

I would spend all day trying to block out the sounds, trying not to think about the jumpy castle, but it was right there, a few feet from my bedroom window, belching out children, then consuming more. Big children and little children and teenagers bounced around in the bloated thing, cackling, shrieking, injuring each other. The madness went on into the wee hours, all of the kids staying up past midnight. The jumpy castle reduced life down to its most essential elements: screaming, laughter, sobbing.

I was afraid of the jumpy castle, afraid of what it would do to my life when it found its way into my yard. *It was so close.* I knew that it would boil me down to my essence, all of the extras evaporating off me like useless gas. No more cold cans of beer, no more escaping whoever is inside the house, no more savoring the day at your own leisure. And also no more dive bars, no more spontaneous road trips, no more talking to my dog like she was my child, no more dancing to the Pixies, no more ass pants, no more high-fiving, no more nonsense. Once you had kids, you no longer had the luxury of staring at the ceiling listening to Radiohead for hours, or eating Girl Scout cookies in bed while watching *Temptation Island.*

Once you entered the jumpy castle, you couldn't stand on the sidewalk in your underwear. You couldn't tell your one neighbor that your other neighbor was crazy. You would have to play nicely with others. You would have to pretend. You would have to jump, for the sake of the family. If you got tired and gave up, everyone around you would keep jumping and you'd fall down and get trampled. Once you enter the jumpy castle, you have to keep jumping, no matter what.

∞

I saw mothers everywhere I went back then, jumpy women with uneasy smiles when they talked to me, like they'd left cookies burning in the oven at home and they really needed to go.

The jumpy women couldn't focus. They were too busy. They had snotty noses to wipe. They had bills to pay. They had groceries to buy. They had pointless, repetitive questions to answer. They were late for work. Or they left work early, but they were still behind. If they didn't have jobs, they were maybe even *jumpier*, because they had more time to feel guilty about half-assing something, screwing something up, overlooking something important. They were jumpy because they were always surrounded by small people who needed their help. Someone was missing her ballet lesson, someone was doing badly in math, someone didn't know how to share, someone wasn't saying please, someone peed the bed, someone's socks and underwear were on the floor.

These women had Tupperware containers filled with Cheerios stuffed into their purses. They had shopping lists and teething rings and sippy cups in there, too, and they were running late. They were always running behind, always forgetting something.

I didn't want to be one of them. I wanted to remain wrapped up in myself, like I'd always been. It was easy being me, finally, after thirty-four years. My underemployed, noncommittal stoner boy-friend had moved out and moved on. I had a decent career, and then I finally had a real, adult boyfriend who truly loved me and showed it every single day. We spent most of our limited time to-gether in bed, having sex or eating something delicious or watching TV or all of the above. I wanted to stay where I was. I didn't want to compete with anyone over the quality of goody bags I handed out at birthday parties. I didn't want to be friendly and helpful all the time. I didn't want to write thank-you notes. I didn't want to be forced to appear grateful or organized yet. No one depended on me. I was determined to remain irresponsible. Bill had a kid across town, but when he was with me, he got to indulge himself in my irresponsible world. Why not? No one was missing breakfast, cry-ing in their room, wandering lost somewhere in the neighborhood.

I had nothing to prove anymore, because I didn't fit in, and I finally understood that I never would. Once you had kids, though, you *had* to fit in, for the sake of someone who couldn't make friends well, someone who didn't know how to cooperate or compromise yet, someone who got shy easily. You had to be a contributing mem-ber of society, because otherwise someone would think it was okay to be withdrawn and grumpy and listen to Dr. Dre even though he rapped about how bitches ain't shit but hos and tricks. A child was likely to be confused by this. Jumpy women never risked confusing anyone, especially a small person who was already struggling with her identity, wondering if she was beautiful, wondering if she was or wasn't a princess.

Maybe I was the one who didn't want to cooperate or compro-mise. Women with kids had to be good role models. They couldn't talk shit about their self-centered friends. They couldn't whine to their husbands about how they didn't feel like doing the dishes right now or ever. They couldn't lie on their couches reading crappy magazines all day just because they felt like it.

If there was one thing a jumpy woman didn't have time for, it was self-pity. Maybe she was driving somewhere in her car, lost in thought, wondering if she was really the same woman who could once command the room at a party. She didn't go to that many parties anymore. People didn't listen as closely to moms. Moms were too wound up about their children to be interesting. Who made them that way, though? Why did the kids at home always make the moms look bad, but somehow the dads got to be the same people they were before they had kids?

No wonder the jumpy women looked tired. They looked like they'd lost something along the way, but they couldn't even remember what it was. And anyway, there was never time to reflect on such things. Someone small was waiting for them to get home.

The morning after the party next door, my backyard was littered with Coke cans and gum wrappers. The neighbor kids liked to throw stuff into my yard. Maybe they were trying to hit something. The dogs? The metal chairs, to make a satisfying clanking sound?

At the grocery store or movie theater or park, when little kids wandered over to me and their moms smiled with pride, I always winced. Toddlers always struck me as unsanitary, like cockroaches. Their hands always looked dirty. Their noses were always crusted in snot. They always seemed to be grabbing at me, invading my personal space, yanking away my car keys or pulling my hair. Or they'd hand me a toy, and then they'd want it back immediately. *What is the point to this game?* I always wondered. Kids made me nervous. I just wanted them to go away.

But sometimes I did watch them, from a safe distance, the schoolkids next door or my friends' toddlers, zigzagging around frantically in my backyard, shrieking, stripping down, prancing around naked, sticking their filthy mitts into the guacamole, then running it all over their bodies.

Kids ruined everything. I didn't find them amusing. I saw only flaws. I didn't like the way that one dressed. I didn't like the look on this one's face. I didn't like the tone this one was taking with his mother, who was obviously trying her best in her own jumpy-woman way.

I didn't realize how much internalized misogyny was wrapped up in my perception of women of all stripes, not just mothers. The truth was, I found fault with most of the women I encountered in the world. Every single one of them looked like a cautionary tale of what *not* to become. I didn't realize yet that I was huffing the patriarchal spray paint that made every woman's life look like a series of big mistakes. All I knew was that I *hated* the voice that mothers used, all big and bright, instructing their kids, *Use your words!* over and over again, as if it weren't obviously more expedient just to use your fists. That voice always seemed to grow louder and louder the more a jumpy woman talked. It was as if she was broadcasting her helpful instructions to everyone on the playground, or everyone on the plane: USE YOUR WORDS! Like she was trying to tell the whole world, SAY PLEASE, PLEASE! and PLEASE SAY THANK YOU, PLEASE! and THANK YOU FOR SAYING THANK YOU!

I didn't want to use my fucking words. I didn't want to cock my head and listen like a trained dog, like they did, every second of their fucking lives, for the sound of screaming, or laughter, or sobbing.

I picked up the last piece of trash and surveyed the yard, trying to decide whether to mow the grass today or walk the dogs instead. Next door, the jumpy castle lay in a deflated heap on the pavement.

The children were gone. The world was quiet again. The wind chimes from my neighbor's backyard jingled in the breeze.

Bill brought Zeke over on a Sunday in the spring, after we'd been dating for six months. Zeke walked into our house, all big round eyes and sharp elbows, sandy blond hair in waves around his cute face, pulsing with that fidgety energy that's so specific to nine-year-olds (hence the fidget spinner). My dog Potus, only a year old then, stood up on her hind legs, batting her paws in the air. She recognized Zeke's puppy vibes immediately. Jangling limbs and ringing laughter! Finally, someone to play with! Zeke took another step and slid across the dining room floor—his shoes had wheels on them. As he spun around in tight circles, Potus chased him, barking happily. *This boy has supernatural powers! A worthy playmate, at long last!*

But my throat tightened up, my hands clenched. *He's going to break something!* Bill and I had already agreed that our relationship was serious. We decided that before I even met Zeke. I had to love him. It was mandatory. But mostly what I thought was: *Here is a human who will be in my life forever and ever.* It made me feel heavy, like I should try to sneak out the back door and maybe go have a drink somewhere while Zeke and his father did their father-son things.

The immediate imperative to love a small stranger made me uncomfortable. *Refusing to love him means you're a bad person*, I told myself. But what if I happened to merely like him? Did I have a choice? I mean, he was pleasant enough. He was smart and nice and seemed to have a good sense of humor. But he was still a kid.

I assumed that when I had my own kids, I would like them. That's what my mom always said, and I didn't doubt her. I wanted to be a good friend and a good stepmother to Zeke, too, eventually. I wanted us to feel like a family. I just didn't want Zeke to step straight into the center of our passionate, deliriously fun romance at that exact moment and mess everything up. All Bill and I knew how to do was lie around in bed. How could a nine-year-old fit into this? The answer was: He couldn't.

Suddenly our present and our future seemed much more difficult. And when the future looks like a tangled web of mysteries, most of them frightening, that's when dread becomes a fixture inside your body. Pessimism sprouts from dread, telling you that whatever comes next, it won't be good, or sweet, or relaxing. It will be hard, and scary.

Dread asks you how much you can handle. Dread tells you you're too weak for these dark obstacles. Dread makes you forget how capable you are, underneath the shivering and the cowering. The only cure for dread is surrender. You banish dread by announcing: *Whatever comes next, I will welcome it with an open heart.*

∞

A month after we got back from Europe, we converted my TV room into a second bedroom for Zeke. That felt very mature and stable, to change the room where my slacker ex-boyfriend used to do bong hits and watch the Tour de France in the middle of the night into a room where a *real* child would sleep and play and do his other (hopefully very quiet) little-kid things.

Not unlike my ex-boyfriend, I viewed Zeke as a small friend or a very interesting pet. But I wasn't sure what my role in his life should be. Zeke already had a mother. That actually made it easier. I didn't have to aim for that kind of solemn responsibility. Instead, I decided to aim for Immature Woman Who Likes Board Games a Lot.

But Zeke sometimes seemed more like a small stranger than a small friend. His erratic, clunky movements through the house felt unpredictable and jarring. There were clomping footsteps in the hallway. There were slammed doors. Zeke sang and talked to himself and made a crazy amount of noise just moving around in his room. It was cute, and it was also unnerving. His presence made my house—now *our* house—feel cozier, but also a tiny bit crowded.

My irritation made me feel incredibly guilty. Why couldn't I be more like Potus, who loved Zeke at first sight? Why wasn't I more of a natural mother, nurturing and sweet?

$$\infty$$

My solution to the problem of Zeke and the problem of disliking children in general was to get pregnant as soon as possible. I would prove that underneath my ambivalent exterior, I was nurturing and sweet. Like pumpkins and mice magically turning into a driver and stagecoach, Zeke would become the helpful big brother, Bill would become the doting daddy, and I would become the loving mommy, all before the stroke of midnight.

I was thirty-five years old and worried about my fertility. I'd spent years hearing about the perils of trying to bear a child in your late thirties, both from my obstetrician sister and a sexist culture hell-bent on scaring women into believing that having all the stuff you wanted—a career, kids, a husband, a life—was impossible, selfish, and doomed. So as soon as Bill and I got engaged, I went off the pill.

I figured it would take a while to get pregnant. I booked a spot for our wedding and called my friend Veronica to tell her about the place I chose—a cute little mom-and-pop hotel in Palm Desert with lots of grass and a big pool surrounded by rooms.

Veronica was alarmed by the fact that I'd gone off the pill. "You can't get pregnant right now! How are you going to plan a wedding when you're pregnant? You'll lose your mind! You have a full-time job, and you're going to be vomiting all the time."

My heart started to race. What was I thinking? So that night I told Bill we'd better be more careful.

One week later, I was pregnant. True to Veronica's prophecy, I felt exhausted and ill and I couldn't think about wedding food without wanting to throw up. Every time I tried to choose appetizers for the wedding, I felt nauseated. Fried olives? Who ever heard of such a repulsive thing? Smoked salmon? Why did that sound so foul and slimy now? All creamy things sounded curdled. All meaty things sounded rancid. All I wanted to serve at the wedding was fresh fruits and vegetables.

"Do you think people will be annoyed if we just serve salads at our wedding?" I asked Veronica, who I'd taken to calling every few hours. She'd just gotten engaged herself, so our existential crises were perfectly in sync.

"Just a salad? Nothing else?"

"Well, maybe a salad and then a fruit salad and then some kind of light, refreshing dessert."

"No. People expect to really *eat* at weddings. There are going to be kids there, right? They have to eat something or they'll freak out. They won't eat salad."

"Fucking kids," I said. "Why do there have to be kids there? I can't believe I'm having a kid soon."

"You already have a kid, actually. But I agree, kids are the worst." Veronica wanted kids too, and she didn't like them either.

So I lay on the couch and stared at the ceiling and Veronica and I discussed the pointlessness of procreating at great length. We listed all the stuff we hated about kids—how they were always leaving their fucking juice boxes everywhere, and they were always repeating themselves and making everything boring, and they were always filling up their parents' houses with ugly plastic bullshit, plus they weren't cute but everyone thought they were, probably because most people were fucking stupid or overcome by hormones or something. And even though I was clearly overcome by hormones myself, grumpy and itchy and murderous inside in distinct, early-pregnancy ways that I wouldn't recognize until my next pregnancy, it felt good to lie there, all queasy and pregnant, going on and on about how *revolting* it was to even consider children and babies and childbirth.

"In a few months, you won't recognize me anymore. I'll be huge. And then after that, you'll never hear from me again. You'll wonder where I went, but I'll be right here, making mac and cheese for some little asshole."

"Oh my god."

"And in a few years, you'll finally see me again, but I'll have gray hair and a huge ass and there'll be a Dora jumpy castle in my backyard."

"A jumpy castle! Jesus Christ, no."

∞

But as Veronica had pointed out, I was already a parent. I was just in denial about it.

Zeke and I were never sure of what to talk about or do together, so we played Monopoly a lot. Luckily, I loved Monopoly and so did Zeke. It was one of the only things we had in common. I particularly loved the first part of the game, when you try to get everything you want and figure out what your fate will be. But I also loved bargaining for other people's properties. I loved plotting my path toward victory: How might I trick this boy and this man into allowing me to crush them one more time?

But even as I was beating Zeke at Monopoly over and over, I was also trying to teach him to play the game as mercilessly as I played it. "You have to buy property immediately," I'd say. "Buy everything. Don't save your money. You can mortgage things if you need cash for houses. Buy as many houses as you can, as soon as possible." Zeke never listened, and neither did Bill. But unlike Zeke, Bill always seemed to have shitty luck. He got sullen when he was losing, but he also bent the rules so Zeke wouldn't get too discouraged. He wasn't brutal enough to win.

But *I* was.

One afternoon, toward the end of a particularly rough game, Zeke started to see that he had no chance of winning, yet again. This was his sixth or seventh big loss to me. I could see a light going on behind his eyes: *This game is just a sadistic form of punishment. It is not a game at all.* Or maybe that light was: *This woman is just a sadistic, selfish human being. She is not a parent at all.*

Zeke landed on one of my hotels on a pink property. "Just mortgage your reds, you don't need them right now," I told him.

"I'm just going to lose," he said, accurately summarizing the situation. "I quit."

"You can't quit," I said. "That's not how you play this game. You have to play to the end."

This is where things get a little tragic. Bill and I were both raised Catholic, by parents firmly focused on turning us into hard-working soldiers. We were hard on ourselves and each other. We believed in toughness and never giving up.

Zeke started crying. This put Bill in a rough spot as a parent: Back your sadistic wife, or your not-all-that-resilient child? Was this a good lesson for your wife or your son, or should you just throw this wretched game out the window right now and never look back?

But Bill and I believed that small windows of suffering were good for a child. We *both* had an empathy chip missing. And when tears entered the picture, that triggered some kind of bad nervous system response that made us both double down on whatever pointlessly rigid position we'd arbitrarily taken at the start. This was the shape a lot of our early parenting took: two merciless people, panicking and doubling down.

Eventually, we softened up and loosened up. But in that moment, Bill backed my play and told Zeke he couldn't quit.

By then, we had an agreement that I wouldn't be enforcing any rules except in the mildest, most back-seat-quarterback sort of way. Zeke didn't need another parent stepping in and telling him how to be, particularly since that parent was also a selfish child who hadn't grown up yet and didn't know a goddamn thing about parenting. This was maybe one of the best decisions we made. Zeke would've resented me a lot if I'd marched around telling him what to do.

But it also meant that when things got difficult, I stepped away and let Bill handle it. I didn't really explain my own position or my feelings as much as I might've if I'd acted more like a real parent. And kids are smart. It probably felt a little dishonest that some initiatives that clearly came from me were being handed down by someone else. Kids prefer transparency. Maybe we all do.

So as Bill told Zeke he couldn't quit, I went to the bathroom. In the bathroom, I stared at the bathroom rug and thought, *Let the kid win, stupid. That's what your mom would do, right? Why do you even care about winning against a nine-year-old? Wouldn't it feel great to cheer him up? Make some bad decisions so he can see how it feels to win for a change.*

By the time I returned, Zeke's face was red and his eyes were squinty, but he had stopped crying. He had resolved to finish the game. Now all I had to do to make things better was give him some of my property outright. *I could give him some money and not call it a loan this time,* I thought.

But. I mean. How would he ever learn how to win at Monopoly if I did that? And shouldn't a kid be able to finish a game without *crying*, for fuck's sake? Didn't *I* have to learn that the hard way? Didn't it make me more competitive, more determined to win at any cost?

Toughness is often the refuge of people who view themselves as inherently bad. *I show myself no mercy, so you won't know mercy, either.* Many of us trick ourselves by claiming that our punishing attitudes toward our kids are all about cultivating grit. But no one gets more resilient just from having a chorus of disparaging sounds implanted inside their heads. Bill and I were teaching Zeke how to beat himself up constantly, the way we did.

And it turns out to be extremely dissatisfying to win against a kid who's just been crying his eyes out. But I was so used to focusing on winning that I couldn't seem to recalibrate. Or maybe stacking up hotels on the orange and pink properties and then watching Bill and Zeke go from hopeful to glum was just one way I had of holding them both at arm's length. Plus I kept telling them they were making bad choices as they made bad choices. No wonder they didn't listen. Winning was my way of punishing them for being bad learners.

But winning was also my way of staying young and bratty and irresponsible. Winning was my way of standing around in my underwear on the sidewalk, smelling the oleander and imitating garbage trucks backing up. I wasn't *just* declaring my independence, I was announcing my total commitment to never playing along nicely, never asking someone to say please, never becoming the shape of a hand yapping, never becoming a jumpy woman.

I never became Zeke's mother, either. I refused to engage with him as a superior, but I also avoided talking through his emotions with him. I didn't realize it then, but I was afraid of getting in too deep. And to be fair, there were plenty of benefits to this for both of us. We focused on playing games, wrestling with the dogs, and talking about *Star Wars*. I tried hard not to chime in when he got in trouble. His mom lived with her girlfriend, and she eventually became his other stepmother. It seemed like overkill to become Mother #3.

But it can also be hard to resist holding the people you love at arm's length. Sometimes you fear possibility itself: the possibility of growing into something more expansive and generous than you are now, growing into a shape that might look ugly from the outside but feels beautiful from the inside.

I had freely chosen to marry a man with a child. But it felt safer to avoid investing in that life. I didn't want to look stupid to my younger self. I didn't want to overinvest in the people who loved me a little too much already.

Somehow, it even felt safer to believe that I was unworthy of anyone's love. Love, like Monopoly, seems to boil down to raw luck, once you subtract the brutality out of the picture. Who wants to remain vulnerable to the whims of fate? Who wants to admit that in marriage, as in Monopoly, you don't know how it will end, but you can never, ever quit?

Sometimes you just want to stand on the sidewalk in your underwear instead. Stand on the sidewalk and tell the world you will always disappoint them. Stand on the sidewalk and please yourself.

PART II

5

Wedlocked

On the day you get everything you've ever wanted, you might feel like you don't deserve it. I assumed that I would rise to the occasion on my wedding day. I believed that true love would deliver me from my neurotic, disheveled self and I would blossom into a heavenly creature—glossy-lipped, graceful, and flawless as a magazine bride. *Today is my day to shine!* I told myself. Yet there I was on my wedding day, sweating and hissing commands instead of floating around on a cloud of fairy dust.

When expectations are sky-high, shame always burns more brightly than pride, at least for me. We'd rented out a small hotel in Palm Desert, California, where we could get married on a grassy lawn, under tall palm trees, next to a swimming pool. Our guests could stay at the hotel together, with their kids. I'd always wanted a wedding that felt like a vacation. But being the center of attention triggered my shame, and my shame told me that I was unworthy of this absurd pageant, this pomp, this fluff, this indulgent frippery. Even though I'd always wanted to get married and have a wedding, those desires felt a little dumb and demeaning. And when we arrived at the hotel, I suddenly felt embarrassed by myself: I was three months pregnant, big and round, and so stupid, and weddings were *also* very stupid! No one *normal* would go to so much hassle just to make an emotional spectacle of themselves in front of everyone they knew.

To be fair, love itself embarrasses me. I'm a daydreamer and a romantic who spent her childhood being told that these things were silly. My family was always allergic to showy displays of positivity or affection. Just being myself, in my family, was embarrassing.

I knew it would be a tough day, so I tried to be practical and anticipate trouble. I hired someone to do my hair and makeup, but my desert-dwelling stylist made my hair look absurd, with chunky ringlets and wilty white roses stuck randomly around my head like obese lice. After an hour of fussing, I looked like a dorky teenager on prom night. I had recruited my close friends to accompany me and prevent bad style choices, but they got bored quickly and ran off to find lunch. I felt abandoned. Tears started smearing my heavy makeup. My friend's extremely stoned husband, the only one left behind, kept snapping photos of me as I cried.

Once I was back in the sterile chill of our hotel room, trying to touch up my face, I knew I would never be sufficiently beautiful. It seemed distasteful to me, to be so pregnant underneath my ludicrous white dress, all primped and powdered, with bad hair starchily sprayed into place. I looked like an overwrapped present—hormonal, overwhelmed, underslept, jittery, full of dread.

Big events have a certain way of unearthing all of my self-hatred. I never wanted bridesmaids, but back in our hotel room, I finally understood their function. Someone should've been there to reassure me. Why had I waved my friends away when they stopped by and offered to hang out? Still, if my friends truly loved me, wouldn't they have insisted on staying?

"Why did I do this?" I asked myself as I looked in the mirror. "What were we thinking?"

There was no father to walk me down the aisle, but if he were still alive, he would've asked me the same question: "Why did you fall for this spectacle?" No one was more cynical about love than he was. What did he say after I moved out of the apartment I'd been sharing with my boyfriend from college? "Playing house is hell."

Playing house, playing bride. A lifetime of heteronormative fantasies rendered me vulnerable, infiltrating every pore, commandeering my cells, so that once I was stricken with the wedding bug, I became unrecognizable to myself. Every unique, thoughtful, nontraditional, nonpatriarchal urge or notion I ever had dissolved into a haze of white—puffy white dresses and cakes and tablecloths and napkins. I'd bought a hot-pink drop-waist gown months earlier, a nontraditional flag of freedom that said, *I am not some man's virginal property acquisition.* But the week of the wedding, my flag of freedom made me look like a bloated child in a pink nightgown. So two days before the wedding, I rushed out to find a traditional white dress with boning to create the illusion of a figure. "Mmmm, much better," I cooed at myself in the bridal boutique mirror. "Now I look like some man's virginal property acquisition."

It was like an out-of-body experience. I also felt exhausted and slightly sick around the clock, as one often does during the first trimester. I couldn't think about the caterer's menu without feeling ill, so Bill and Zeke had driven out to the desert to taste samples of the caterer's food and make selections for us. A nine-year-old chose my wedding menu.

Nothing made sense. It went beyond the food. I wanted our friend's rock band to learn a long list of songs I assigned to them. I wanted to sing one of the songs myself, a choice that's excusable for, say, your sister who's an actress. But for a large pregnant woman, bedazzled like a Christmas ornament, singing at your own wedding is a very bad look indeed. How can I even explain? I was all hopped up on pregnancy hormones, at once aggravated and manic. I wanted things I'd never wanted before or since. I needed things I'd previously thought were stupid. I demanded things I didn't understand a few days later. A wedding is the culmination of every wrongheaded notion you've ever had, every delusional belief you've ever embraced, every self-obsessed urge you've ever indulged: You be the prince, and I'll be the princess. You be the mommy, I'll be the daddy. You be the groom, I'll be the knocked-up bride.

It didn't help that Bill's sister kept looking down at my stomach when I greeted her at the hotel.

"You know I'm pregnant, right?" I asked her.

"Oh wow! Congratulations!" she said with a nervous laugh. "I was kind of wondering if you'd put on weight!"

Incredible, I thought. *Bill didn't even tell his family ahead of time.* Now I would have to break the news to them, one by one. How relaxing. And no matter what I said, they'd probably just assume that the pregnancy was unplanned and I'd tricked Bill into marrying me. *Welcome to your shotgun wedding, princess.*

Bill had finally proposed to me on Christmas Eve. I had told him that he should propose on some ordinary day, just the two of us at a nice restaurant, very private, no big scenes, no being put on the spot in front of a crowd. I also told him, at least three or four times, "Whatever you do, don't propose to me on Christmas." I didn't want my family there, and I didn't want to associate my engagement with a big holiday. But by then it was becoming apparent that Bill didn't have any long-term memory to speak of. Fifteen years later, I know that if I want to prevent him from doing something, I have to warn him five minutes before he's most likely to do it. That's a very small window of opportunity, but that's how people who only have short-term memories operate. Bill's lack of a functioning frontal lobe was just one of many haunting deficits I had discovered over the course of our first year together, but it was definitely the most unnerving one. I was about to pledge my life to a chapter out of Oliver Sacks's *The Man Who Mistook His Wife for a Hat*.

Christmas dinner was almost on the table, but Bill told my mother that we needed to take a quick walk. That sounded rude to me, until I saw the self-conscious smile on my mother's face and realized that he might've already asked her for my hand in marriage, of all horrifying things. My father had died eleven years earlier, so if Bill wanted to make our big moment into an archaic transactional formality, my mom was the ticket.

"We're about to eat," I hissed at Bill, standing in the middle of the living room, where everyone else was seated. I hated his tucked-in plaid shirt and his bad, pleated khaki pants. Khakis with pleats! Who beamed in this 1980s-era nightmare dad? I hated my baggy corduroy pants and my shapeless gray sweater. These were not Getting Engaged clothes!

"We really should take a walk," Bill said, looking deeply unlovable. I hated Bill's dumb face and I hated my family watching silently and I hated Christmas itself. But I couldn't fight right there, in front of everyone. I needed to play along. Bill looked like he felt sick, which made me feel a tiny bit sorry for him.

I probably should've felt relieved. It was finally obvious that this guy was going to fuck our engagement straight into the ground no matter what I said or did. Getting engaged with my family there was like trying to do water ballet in a tank full of piranhas. Everyone would wait around for us to tell them what they already knew. Just seeing their strained smiles filled me with despair.

My stomach was roiling as we left the house. Bill didn't really like romantic gestures that much. I was starting to realize that I didn't like them either. As an adult, they just made me feel awkward. I wanted to find the romance in ordinary moments. That was why I kept trying to give Bill plenty of instruction: I didn't want us to be disappointed by ourselves and each other. I hated feeling like big moments always had to be a letdown.

We crossed the street and walked down into the grass of the public golf course next to my house, headed nowhere. I wanted to fix the mood, make a joke or something, but I had to stay very quiet just to prevent myself from saying something shitty. I didn't want my memory of our engagement to be framed by some snippy remark.

Then suddenly, Bill stopped and turned to me with a jerk and said, "As you know, we've known each other for a long time now ..."

As you know. I was incredulous. I have never loved Bill less than I did in that moment. I looked at him with dead eyes as meaningless words flowed out of his mouth. I'd tell you the rest, but I sort of half blacked out after that. I was getting engaged to a broken robot.

I knew, intellectually, that I wanted to spend my life with him. The year and a half we'd spent together had been so easy, and so relaxing, and so satisfying—at least when we were alone. But we didn't have much practical experience as a couple out in the world. And under duress, we were both stress cases. Even though Bill was good at tackling some calamities, he was bad at playing a role, and awful at aping confidence. He cannot act or pretend or lie to save his life. And when he gets nervous and I get overly critical, we both stop functioning entirely and we lose our tempers. At our worst, we're a warehouse packed with gun powder.

I still said yes, sure, of course, and we kissed quickly. But as we turned around and walked back to the house, I knew for the first time that Bill would never stop tormenting me with his nerves and his bad judgment. I felt like an asshole, but I knew, viscerally, that we were in for a rough ride.

∞

Bill was in our hotel room now, talking about chairs that need to be moved out of the sun because we're in the desert and it's 107 degrees outside. The groom has seen the bride before the wedding, but the bride and groom don't believe in bad luck. Maybe they should, though.

The phone rang. Steve, my friend who was marrying us, told me that the microphone wouldn't work because they'd moved the chairs to the shade and the mic cord wouldn't stretch that far.

"Okay, I'll send Bill out there," I told him. Then I turned to Bill. "Make them sit in the sun. We need the microphone. No one will hear a word without it." We'd written our own vows. Of all of the stupid choices we'd made, those words were the only thing that made sense, the only thing that mattered.

"It is *extremely hot* out there," Bill said, as if I, a pregnant lady, were unaware of such things.

"Let them sit in the fucking sun," I growled.

"I'll see what I can do," Bill said. I did not like the noncommittal sound of this. It was almost as if he didn't respect my authority *as the motherfucking bride.*

"We need the mic, Bill. It's *important.*" I'd been to weddings where you couldn't hear a thing. Everyone assumed they didn't need a mic, but they always did. As Bill left, I fixed him with a weighty look. "Trust me on this, please."

But we weren't married yet, so he still thought he could do whatever he wanted. Bless his heart. Inside his glorious head there were no long-term memories, and that left extra room for his imagination. His imagination had been telling him for decades that he could follow his own whims wherever they led. Even though he was about to get married, he still believed that he had free will because we'd spent the past eighteen months eating Thai food and watching *The Wire.* He had some inkling that I was a little intense by then, but he had no idea how much I sweated the small stuff. He didn't realize how much I sweated, *period.* He was about to find out.

The phone rang again. It was showtime. I was all alone. *Why did we do it like this?* I tried to focus on standing up straight. *Everything that happens around you is a manifestation of your confusion.*

You are too weak and too conflicted for bold gestures and grand procla-
mations. Everything you try is an embarrassment.

∞

As I walk down the path to where our guests are waiting, my legs immediately begin dripping with sweat. I have what feels like a down comforter strapped to my body. Zeke is playing the wedding march on his keyboard. He segues into "The Imperial March" from *Star Wars*. The crowd believes that he's messing up. They don't get the joke.

Why are we making jokes, again? Oh yes, because I am Darth Vader, cleverly disguised as Princess Leia. I am a threat to this in-nocent boy, a threat to the whole galaxy. Our jokes are too real, as always.

Then Bill spots me from far away and looks at me like I am not scary or repellent. Odd, I think, how happy he looks to see me.

Steve begins to speak, without a microphone. I look out at the rows of people watching. The first two rows are smiling. The next five rows are squinting at us, uncomprehending. They can't hear a thing.

Bill didn't listen. He said "Fuck it" and did what he wanted in-stead. And isn't it fitting that I should realize, a few minutes before becoming officially married, that once you merge your fate with the fate of another, you have no control over your circumstances? Because even after years of careful training, a spouse will still do whatever a spouse feels like doing. You may have omitted the word *obey* from your wedding vows, but you have been quietly expecting obedience nonetheless. Obedience is a prerequisite for you, in fact, if you're going to pledge your body to another human being until death. Your body and soul will be his, sure, but only in exchange for total acquiescence. That was the deal you thought you were making.

And in that sweat-soaked moment, I discovered that my subconscious expectation would be a never-ending farce. Because standing there, on the grass, in the blazing sun, with one hundred and three people watching but most of them not hearing a word, I realized that my husband would *never* obey—and neither would I.

Getting what you want necessitates believing that you deserve it. You have to *choose* to believe that. Getting means having. Having means holding. Holding means forgiving, over and over again. At the start of the ceremony I felt self-conscious and annoyed. I hated me and us. And then Bill started saying his vows and I started crying and everything shifted, re-sorting our cells, realigning the stars.

As tears poured down my cheeks in oily black mascara streaks, I looked out at our guests. The first two rows were crying, and the next five rows were still just squinting—unmoved, uncomprehending. *It's just as well*, I thought. Did it really matter?

Next I forgave the caterer for putting two random red grapes on each plate, like some cheap garnish that rolled around pointlessly. I forgave myself for chugging two nonalcoholic beers in a row with our meal, which apparently confused Bill's sister, who thought I was pregnant and pounding drinks anyway. I forgave myself for making a ridiculously regressive speech, something about the luck of finding a man at the age of thirty-four.

When I met Bill's nieces, ages six and eleven, I forgave them for telling me that I was their aunt. This felt heavy for some reason. My responsibilities as a human were starting to pile up, but I forgave myself for feeling oppressed by the word *aunt*. I did not want to serve as some sort of matriarchal-adjacent figure to these small, chatty strangers. My heart was three sizes too small. Who knew? *Forgiven!*

Then my mother gave a toast that began with these exact words: "Well, we're all a little tired of weddings, to be honest." I laughed loudly at this, that's how expansive I was feeling at the time. Bill laughed, too, and didn't look stricken at all, much to his credit. For years to come, Bill's relatives would lament how awful my mother's toast was. My mother would adamantly insist that she did *not* say those words, another signature move of hers. Luckily, there were 103 witnesses.

My mom's joke doesn't sound all that funny to me now, fifteen years later. But in that moment, I was relieved. My mom's grumpiness represented the essence of what a wedding *should* be: two messed-up families, trying very hard to honor the newlyweds and mostly failing. When everyone else is being a little too gushingly positive, my mom feels it's her duty to offer up a little darkness, a punch line, something to bring reality back into the picture for a second.

My mother is also a little bit like Bill: she *hates* being forced to play a role for an audience. But instead of getting nervous and making arbitrary robot sounds, she shifts into a dismissive tone, and blurts things out that are inappropriate or downright brutal. My strange affliction is that I toggle between Bill's ineptitude, my mom's harshness, and my own occasional geyser of love and affection, which is how I went from seeing the wedding as an enormous mistake to thinking it was the best thing I'd ever done in a few minutes flat. The cathartic stress of the day cleared the way for the ecstatic bliss of the reception: Bill was my dream man! My mother was delightful and quirky! Every human alive was lovable and perfect! I had transformed into a supernaturally adoring princess bride at last.

I could finally see the point to all of that planning. I was grateful for those witnesses and grateful for that obscene spectacle. I was thrilled to have dragged everyone straight to hell with us.

So I got up and sang "Martinis on the Roof" by Superchunk and people sort of half watched, embarrassed for me, and then there were drunk people milling around and toddlers on the dance floor and kids in the pool, and finally my mom and my siblings went back to their rooms at the other hotel and my close friends stayed and drank more, and then Bill and I returned to our room, awash in relief and gratitude.

"I'm so glad we did this," Bill said. He meant the wedding, not the marriage. He meant the expense and the hassles, all of it.

"Me, too," I said, "So glad!" We lay across the bed, grinning at each other, and talked happily about how overwhelming it all felt. We kissed and talked and kissed some more. We felt extremely lucky, almost *dangerously* lucky. Outside we could hear our guests, our witnesses, shouting and drinking and dancing under the twinkling desert stars.

On the day you get everything you've ever wanted, you might just feel so grateful for all of it that you can hardly sleep. Your head is awash with the faces of your closest friends and relatives, gathered in one place. Your heart is full of devotion to them, to your brand-new stepson, to your brand-new nieces, to your mother, and to your husband—your brand-new husband, a patient, beautiful man who's a million times better than any other man you've ever met. You might be the luckiest woman alive.

Maybe it will always be like this, you think. *Maybe life just gets easier and easier.* You are as naive as a bride should be on her wedding night. You are clueless and you are more in love than you've ever been before. You are poised at the start of your life's most magnificent creation: a two-headed gargoyle, chasing its own tail, disobedient and conflicted. You have set a divine catastrophe into motion.

6

Expecting the Worst

Pregnancy means feeling at once consecrated and cursed. I wake up with a clear sense of my position on the globe. Every cell feels electric. I am pulled forward through my day as if directed by some inner demon—possessed, guided. After a lifetime of mixed feelings about everything under the sun, suddenly there is no ambivalence, no hesitation. I can see the path before me clearly. Every nerve is focused on the future. Light bends around the landscape like it's moving through water. I am the Virgin Mary—serene, expansive, merciful—but I am also prepared to cut down anyone who stands in my way, without a second of doubt.

My body changes each day—ravenous then queasy, exhausted then energized, chilly then overheated—but I know my location for the first time, a blinking white light on the map. A new sense of focus descends on my cells. *This is what you were called to do.*

I don't mean I've been called to have a baby, of course. *What is a baby?* I find myself thinking often. It's pretty hard to picture my baby, even as I'm buying baby things. My baby is still theoretical. What I mean is that I have been called to scrub my entire life clean. I am meant to sterilize the bathrooms, massacre invading flies, scour the internet for an affordable rug for the baby room, reorganize all of my stuff, declutter the world, redesign the universe.

My clarity of purpose is driven by a vague sense of unrest, a frustration with the current state of things. Unseen filth seems to hide in the walls of my house: psychic black mold, emotional asbestos. Meanwhile, sometimes it seems like there is a tyrant growing inside me and it is supernatural, an alien, the Christ child, a restless dictator, a ravenous reptile. Everything needs to be put in order quickly, before my tiny boss arrives: *These dogs need to learn some manners. This boy needs a better haircut. This man . . . Where do we even begin? How do we train this foot soldier for what's to come?*

Now that the terrors of engagement and wedding are safely past, it has become much more obvious that Bill is the best possible husband: thoughtful, helpful, and extremely sympathetic to proclamations like "I am enormous! I feel crazy!" and "I need help finding my keys or I am going to murder someone!" He even runs out to fetch me emergency nachos and extremely time-sensitive milkshakes without complaint.

Even so, I am moving in fast motion, and Bill is very slow. My mind is racing and his seems to be sputtering. On our walks around the Rose Bowl and its neighboring golf course, as I balloon larger and larger each day, I set an aggressive pace and Bill struggles to keep up. I am shaped like Humpty Dumpty now, I have a bowling ball lodged just above my pelvic bone, my groin feels like it's being crushed, but these things only sharpen my focus and quicken my step. I stare straight into the eyes of those who dawdle in my path: *Are you kidding me? Do I look like I'm fucking around?* I am enormous and comically round, but Bill is the clumsy one, lagging behind, mumbling about his bad knees, asking why we're in such a hurry. "This is exercise," I tell him. "We are *exercising.*"

I am manic, jacked up on hormonal meth. I am impatient, enraged, vicious. Then, like an unexpected breeze, the mood shifts. Sunlight curves up from the pavement with a sparkling wink, sweeps through the blue sky: I am effusive and benevolent, a matriarch in waiting. I bestride the narrow world like a colossus.

$$\infty$$

I still don't know a thing about pregnancy. I am a rapidly evolving biological machine without an instruction manual. I try to ask the mothers I know what is in store for me, but the best they can do is tell me to buy a copy of *What to Expect When You're Expecting.* This is like telling someone planning a trip to the beach to rent *Jaws,* or pressing a copy of *The Sheltering Sky* into the hands of someone on their way to Morocco.

Some sharp light inside me still craves knowledge, devastating details, dark omens of ills to come, so I buy a copy of the book. I find myself studying it every night, keeping it on my bedside table, poring over each word of its chilling prophecy. As my body expands, I start to treasure the book's hideous descent into the hell of gestation. I savor its encyclopedic delineation of every malady and gruesome side effect ever experienced by any pregnant woman anywhere. Conveniently, the grotesqueries listed therein, from heartburn to hemorrhoids to chronic dependence on adult diapers, are divided into monthly sections, allowing me to savor a tiny dose of suspense-horror thrills and chills before falling into my simultaneously deep and restless Humpty Dumpty sleep.

Some nights when I know that I've been fully apprised of the vast range of ailments typical of my gestational achievement level, I flip ahead in the book. Like a child on Christmas Eve peeking through a cracked door to get a glimpse of the bounty of gifts waiting under the tree, I marvel at the gory mysteries to come: Heartburn. Stretch marks. Preeclampsia. Prenatal diabetes. Cankles. Something about a "bloody plug."

When Bill and I crawl under our down comforter every night, I don't want to read anything else. I just want to reflect on the freakish roller coaster I've willingly boarded. I want to relish my progress toward the unknown. As the weeks go by and I grow bigger, I spend a solid half hour massaging pricey stretch-mark-prevention cream across my round belly. Bill and I joke that it's made of pig placentas, possibly because it is. It doesn't bother me; it makes simple sense. Every satanic ritual necessitates a sacrifice. The second I forget about what the lotion is made of, my dog Potus crawls up next to me, smelling something very rich, waiting for an opportunistic lick.

Yes, pregnancy is the first step along the path to degradation. The Virgin Mary's air of holiness and benevolent calm yields to depravity and chaos heretofore unknown.

Some nights I don't read a word, I just sit in silence and stare at the cover of *What to Expect When You're Expecting*, marveling at what a con job the publisher has pulled off. The book is pink and yellow and covered in some kind of flocked, flowery wallpaper or quilt pattern meant to evoke a cheerful middle-American setting. What I see on that cover, through the haze of my oddly upbeat but also irritated mood, is one of those overheated split-level homes in the Midwest that have "country" decorations everywhere, from porcelain milkmaid figurines to framed pictures of white ducks with blue ribbons around their necks to wooden bins with the words "Taters 'n' Onions" painted on the top. A mere glance at the cover could induce hot flashes, cramping, and suicidal ideation in any woman of childbearing age.

And that's before my eyes settle on the main illustration. There, perched amid all those tiny yellow and pink flowers, is the expectant mother of every woman's nightmares. On my copy, she has a perky bob haircut, the sort of molded, unmoving hair that only a woman without mirrors in her house would have the audacity to wear outside. She's dressed in a yellow Mr. Rogers–style cardigan and red polyester slacks that call to mind your fourth-grade social studies teacher, the one who gave an entire class of nine-year-olds night sweats by telling them that the Iran hostage crisis was sure to develop into World War III.

The woman has on terrible geriatric penny loafers. She is perched primly in a rocking chair with this filthy, chipper smile on her face, like all she's done for months is sit there, rocking back and forth, only occasionally stopping to peruse the Debilitating Symptom of the Month or to order more whimsical milkmaid figurines for the dining room. You could pass out copies of this image at local high schools and instantly cut the teenage pregnancy rate in half.

It isn't just that the woman's style choices offend. It's that calm look on her face. This is clearly not a person who's been suffering through bouts of heartburn and dizzy spells. This smug mutant is not waking up five times a night to use the bathroom, nor is she struggling with numbness or heart palpitations. This woman is living a lie. She is *not* in her last month of pregnancy. She hasn't been told that she could give birth any second, which is a little like being told that you have a bomb strapped to your chest and only Mother Nature (that bitch!) has access to the trigger. She bears no evidence of having random and unpredictable bouts of hormonal rage (listed merely as "mood swings" in this otherwise ruthless book).

But I know all too well that pregnant women don't sit primly in rocking chairs, looking satisfied with their bad haircuts. No. They drive too fast on the freeway, screeching at passing cars.

In the last months of pregnancy, women don't smile bucolically while folding onesies in the baby room. They obsessively pull weeds out of the front yard while loudly berating their husbands for leaving the back door unlocked and forgetting to get the dog vitamins even though they were *clearly on the list*. The last month of pregnancy doesn't just prepare a woman to squeeze out a child. It prepares her to wage bloody revolution.

$$\infty$$

Thanks to the glory of gestation, the purest rage lives at the heart of my being, and somehow it also feels like the purest joy I've ever experienced. Bill and I have taken to calling it "good mood PMS": constant indignation, with a smile. I am propelled forward by an around-the-clock, buoyant, *energetic* anger. My vibe is not unlike that of a gleeful prepper, one who spends each day busily storing canned goods and ammunition in their basement, secretly giddy about the apocalypse. I recognize that my life is about to be destroyed, but I am *anxious for the destruction to begin*. I just want to make sure everything is perfect before the storm hits. The house needs to be in order. The baby room needs to be ready. We won't have time to fix a thing, once the theoretical baby arrives and our lives descend into chaos. Everything needs to be in its proper place before it's all scattered and pulverized.

I attack every hour of every day. There is too much to do. I am in constant motion.

When I'm in this state, Bill seems almost like a piece of furniture in the room: inert, obstructive, devoid of purpose. So I tell my armchair: *Go to this store. Pick up this order. Return and do the dishes.* My voice always has an edge to it. Even when I'm trying to be friendly, there's a note of *Don't fuck this up* in the mix. My eyes are focused and intense, like a laser strong enough to cut your face off. That's Satan, or the Christ child, or the rapacious lizard in my gut, or the manic dictator at my core. *We need a rack to dry the baby bottles on. No, a special rack, not a regular dish rack. Come on, guy. Wake up.* Bill doesn't nitpick or bicker. Formidable forces are clearly in play here. Better watch your step.

One morning after Bill leaves for work, our two dogs are barking furiously at the back gate. I discover a very small puppy outside, whining to get in. I'm already running late for a doctor's appointment, but I scoop up the puppy and shut her in the bathroom with a bowl of water and some food. This feels like a bad solution, but I can't just leave her outside crying and drive away. I close the doors to the bathroom so the other dogs won't bother her. I figure I'll be back in an hour, and I'll decide how to handle her then.

I'm due to take a fasting cholesterol test at my doctor's office downtown in a few minutes. But really, should a pregnant woman be fasting for any reason whatsoever? Doesn't that cursed book say that your cholesterol goes up when you're pregnant, but it's no cause for concern? Why find out how high it's climbing, if it's only temporary? These are questions I might've asked if my mind were working correctly when I made the appointment. But it's very hard to balance the world's demands against your own imperatives when you're pregnant. Sometimes you're too stubborn. Other times, you surrender way too much.

I feel a tiny bit lightheaded on my drive downtown. The devil has me in his clutches. When I arrive I'm led back to a room, where a nurse stabs my arm repeatedly. I had blood taken from my arm a total of two times before I got pregnant, and now it feels like someone is doing it every other week. I am entering my third trimester and I weigh about a hundred and sixty pounds, a solid twenty pounds over my normal weight and five pounds more than my doctor wanted me to gain. I often feel faint before I eat breakfast in the morning, and this morning I can't have any breakfast at all, and now I am being repeatedly jabbed because the nurse is unable to find a solid vein. I am not good with veins. The word *vein* alone makes me feel faint sometimes. I think of the puppy in the bathroom. I think about the rug for the baby room, the one that hasn't arrived yet. I imagine Bill off at work, walking among the average-sized-and-shaped citizens of the free world, untouched by demons, unburdened by thoughts of preeclampsia and prenatal diabetes.

Another nurse enters and takes over. "No worries," she says, stabbing the top of my hand instead. "No problem." The edges of my vision turn dark. "I might faint," I announce, matter-of-factly.

The nurses recline my chair. They bring me orange juice. Then the physician's assistant enters and announces, "We need to send you to the ICU."

"I faint easily," I tell her. She is not my regular doctor, but for some reason she keeps showing up for my appointments instead. "I don't think I need the ICU. I am very pregnant, and I haven't eaten yet."

"I'm not worried about *you*, I'm thinking about the health of your baby," she says. I look her in the eyes. *She just clearly stated that she doesn't give a fuck about me or my health.* My baby is her primary concern.

I try to imagine the baby for a second. I have met very few babies over the past few years, since I tend to avoid them. I wouldn't recognize my own baby if we were suddenly introduced. Can we be sure that my baby is even a baby? Couldn't it be a bowling ball instead?

This woman seems certain that the bowling ball is a baby. She is scolding me because she feels I'm being reckless with my theoretical baby. I am not nearly as important as the baby. I'm just a giant malfunctioning incubator with legs. Inside my manic, murderous mind, she is letting me know that her job, guarding my baby, is honorable, and that she already loves my baby more than I do because she is a compassionate hero and I am a selfish, bloated piece of trash.

I am at once enraged and lost in self-hating thoughts as they wheel me into the ICU and hook me up to machines. I think about the puppy in the bathroom again. I try to call Bill, but he doesn't answer. I quietly wish, not for the first time, that the baby in my gut might turn out to be a puppy, too. I have met many puppies. I *adore* puppies. I already know that. If the physician's assistant had said "I'm thinking of the health of your puppy," I would've understood her concern completely.

But I'm worried about the puppy at home, too. The air smells like bleach and rubbing alcohol. The white sheet feels rough against my skin. I listen to the beeping of the machines and selfishly wonder if my own heart is functioning properly.

No doctor appears for an hour. Finally a nurse comes in.

"Do you know when a doctor will come?"

"I'm not sure, I can check, but your vitals are completely normal." She says this with a meaningful look, one that quite possibly says, *We know this physician's assistant you're dealing with. We have observed her ways before, perhaps you should scrutinize her choices more thoroughly.*

But I feel shy about speaking up. Speaking up means I'm already a shitty mother. I don't want to appear to be reckless with my theoretical baby. I don't want anyone to figure out that I'm still not convinced that my baby is really a baby.

I'm focused, intense, and ready to engage in fisticuffs if necessary, but I'm not tough like a real mother yet. I'm vulnerable. I still need books to tell me how I should be feeling. I still require authoritative strangers to tell me what to do next. The baby is about to change all of that, very soon. The next baby will change things even more. I will become tougher and tougher, meaner and meaner. I will grow into something even more demonic, even more merciless, on behalf of my babies. Shyness will soon be the least of my concerns. I won't *mind* seeming self-serving and quite possibly possessed, soon enough. But not yet.

No doctor arrives. The physician's assistant doesn't show up either. I start to cry. A nurse comes in. I tell her about the puppy in the bathroom at home, all alone for three hours now. I tell her I can't reach my husband. I tell her I am worried, I am upset, and it can't be healthy for the baby when its giant incubator starts spewing smoke and sparks like this.

"You can leave, you know," the nurse says. "Your vitals are fine. You can just sign yourself out."

"Is that stupid?" I ask.

"I don't think so," she says. "I think you're just pregnant and you didn't eat breakfast."

I get up out of bed and sign the release form. It says something about how it will be my fault if I die. There is no mention of babies in the paperwork. Nothing on the form says that I am a selfish person who will make a terrible mother.

The physician's assistant arrives just as I finish signing out, of course. "What are you doing?" she asks, alarm in her eyes.

"No doctor has even looked at me," I say.

"I was busy, I was on my way," she says.

"All of her vitals are normal and have been for several hours," the nurse says, and I feel a love for this woman that almost makes me cry.

"I'm not worried about you," the physician's assistant says again, looking at me and not the nurse. "I'm worried about your baby."

If I could travel back in time, I would ask her, "Do you think there is a specific problem with the baby? And why *aren't* you concerned about me at all?"

Instead, I tell her, flatly, that I feel fine and I can't stay.

A few weeks later, I return for the results of my test. When the physician's assistant tells me that my cholesterol is very high, and then starts to fill me in on the existence of such things as *nonfat milk* and *nonfat yogurt*, I decide to fill her in on a few things, too. "You know that cholesterol is elevated in women who are pregnant, right?" I say to her. "You know that doctors generally don't advise pregnant women to check their cholesterol, least of all take a fasting test, right? Because the numbers are meaningless and it just stresses everyone out?" She glares at me and says nothing for a beat, then goes right back to talking about the low-fat cheeses that are currently available at my local grocery store. *This woman never reads books,* I think. *She prefers pamphlets. She doesn't even like adults. She prefers babies.*

But it's strange to be viewed as a vessel, as a baby delivery system, as a reckless woman who is imperiling her innocent child. It's like waking up in the middle of *The Handmaid's Tale.* You are not important. You are nothing and no one.

That is also the awful foreshadowing at the heart of the *What to Expect* cover art. This woman, with her bad hair, is inconsequential. Her bad clothing no longer matters. The meaning in her life begins and ends with the bulge in her gut. This is the only worthwhile thing she's ever done and will ever do. This is the one shining moment of her entire life.

She is no longer a sexual being. Her opinions are always overruled by experts who know better. Her job is to smile softly and give the baby what it needs. Her job is to keep the baby alive. In bringing a new person into the world, her own personhood evaporates into thin air. She is more like a cow—a cow with a big job to do.

As a pregnant woman, I am expanding and also disappearing.

Life is about to change dramatically, and I am overcompensating and also trying to hide. I am talking very loudly everywhere I go, but I am also embarrassed by myself, by how big and pregnant and unwieldy I am, by what a strange cliché I've become. People want to touch me, which is exactly what I *don't* want, as an oven with legs, bulky and overheating every few minutes in the middle of a very long, hot summer. People want to make weird proclamations like "You're about to be a MAMA!" I don't like the word *mama*, and I never have. I don't trust that things will work out fine and soon I'll have a baby. I believe that something will probably go wrong. I walk around with that knowledge without daring to put it into words.

My back has started to hurt a lot in my last trimester of pregnancy. Sciatica pains shoot down my leg when I pivot the wrong way. I am starting to get heartburn after dinner. It makes me feel sick and anxious. I feel chest pains and worry that I'm having a heart attack. The only thing that seems to cure that feeling is Fuji apples, nibbled very slowly, and also back rubs. Bill starts giving me back rubs every night, and they're the best part of my day. They're the only thing that makes the pain go away. But I also feel like a great white whale in bed, covered in lotion made from pig placentas. I feel horrifically unattractive.

Bill tells me I look sexy, which feels unhinged, but somehow I trust him when he says it. He tells me that everything will be fine, we will have the baby and it will be great. He's had a baby before. Babies are amazing. They are extremely fun to have around. He makes babies sound like puppies, only even better, because they talk. He makes our life together sound like a carnival ride, like a hilarious experiment, like an adventure. It helps.

Even when I got back from the ICU and let the puppy out of

the bathroom and then Bill came home and I told him the whole story of my bad experience that morning—how I almost fainted and then cried and I couldn't reach him and then I went through the McDonald's drive-thru and ordered two hamburger Happy Meals and ate them on the way home on the freeway, cursing the physician's assistant all the while—he never once doubted my judgment for saving the puppy, or leaving the hospital. He never told me it wasn't smart to be eating salty, greasy fast food, or said anything like "I'm just worried about the baby," or made me feel weak for fainting over a needle.

Instead, he said, "Poor baby!" And finally, I could breathe.

One afternoon during the last month of my pregnancy, I am on the phone with Home Depot and someone informs me that the rug for the baby's room won't be delivered in a week, as promised. Instead, it will arrive at our house three weeks after the baby is born. Unacceptable! Everything else is on track: we placed the puppy with a nice family, the yard is under control, the baby room is almost finished. "My baby will be here in two weeks," I say through gritted teeth. "I cannot be putting a rug in the baby's room once we have an actual baby! It is not possible!"

The person on the phone is not interested in the baby or the baby's room, but the person does notice the edge in my voice. The person passes the phone to another person who is similarly disengaged from the life-or-death stakes of the rug delivery. Finally someone in the rug department seems mildly invested, but then, instead of putting me on hold, she puts the phone down on her desk and then gets up to talk to someone else.

I can hear her talking in the distance. I listen for a while. Is she discussing how important it is that someone find a way to get me the rug sooner? Silence. More chatter. Laughter. These people are not talking about my rug. She has forgotten about me. I am like a tiny person on her desk. She might not notice me for hours. I will need to yell very loud, like the tiny people in *Horton Hears a Who!*, just for her to hear me.

"Helloooooo?" I yell. The chatter continues.

"Hellooooooo?!" I bellow. *"Hellooooooooooooo?!!!!!"*

The faces of Bill and my dog Potus appear in the doorway, looking very afraid. They're hesitant to come any closer. *Please don't kill us.*

"They won't pick up the phone!" I say. "They forgot about me! They put the phone down and they don't even know I'm still here!"

Bill silently takes the phone out of my hands. He waits for the person to answer. He asks about the rug. They agree to speed things up.

One morning a few days later, I am weeping over a yogurt lid that refuses to pull off. I stop and take a deep breath.

"Okay," I say to Bill, "It's official. I am losing my mind."

I walk into the living room and lie down on the couch. Bill follows me and sits down next to me, pulling my feet onto his lap. My face is beet red. I am sweating. My nuclear reactor of a body, in its preparations for squeezing out our first child, is also preparing me to build bombs and wage hand-to-hand combat, if necessary.

"I'm sorry," I tell Bill. The first of many apologies. That's marriage, maybe: A lifetime of apologies to each other, to everyone else, to the trees outside your window, to the shoes on your feet. A lifetime of apologies to your children, your pets, your parents, your friends. "I'm doing my best," you tell them. "I swear, I'm doing my best."

But before I even apologize to Bill, he's already forgiven me. That's often the case, it's not just this time. Maybe he's a sucker for abuse, but I want to say it's healthier than that. When I'm sad, he listens closely and he tries hard to understand. Sometimes I lose sight of everything—myself, my love for him, my car keys, the reason for my existence.

And sometimes Bill does, too, to be fair. In more mundane circumstances, he tends to panic before I do. He overreacts to the kinds of smaller hassles that just make me sharpen my focus and work harder. I am very bad when expectations are running high and something big is about to happen, but Bill is very bad with the tiny little tasks that pop up every day. He looks to me for that *This Is Nothing, Let's Just Get 'Er Done* energy, and I look to him for that *This Big Feeling Is Normal, the Sky Is Not Falling* energy.

He tells me there's no need to be sorry. Soon, we'll be having a baby. Soon, everything will change. It won't be scary or bad. It will be fun and exciting. *This is an adventure*, he tells me. Hope dances into the room like sunshine. We are having an adventure.

7

Just Relax

The baby arrived, and time stopped. The baby was real. The baby was good.

I did not expect this story to end well. My arms were strapped down. My gut was cut open like a fish. I was taking deep breaths. Bill was rubbing my temples. I was talking to myself: *This will be done quickly. We can trust medical science. These doctors know what they're doing. It is very unlikely that this hospital will burn down while I can't move my legs, and even if this hospital does burn down, it is exceptionally unlikely that everyone will run out of the room and forget I'm still lying here, strapped to this table, guts out, fully awake.*

Luckily, someone asked me how I was feeling. "I feel very cold and a little nauseated," I said. The anesthesiologist added something to my IV, and within seconds, I felt warmer and better. *Mmm, the wonders of medicine,* I thought. *I trust doctors.*

I said this to myself often in the home stretch of my pregnancy. Unlike my natural-birth-embracing peers, I reversed everything

I'd learned about the evils of patriarchal gynecology in my early-1990s women's studies courses by reading a single book with a clinical title that boiled down to "Epidurals Are Our Friends." The author of the book advanced the notion that insisting on giving birth without pharmaceutical assistance, particularly over the age of thirty-five, often ends in an arduous, painful struggle that, despite everyone's best efforts, usually concludes with a C-section. The experiences of my friends with babies seemed to support this thesis: After twenty-four hours of labor, the special back rubs are doing no good, the special mixtape long ago wore out its welcome, and everyone is weeping and sweating and begging to be put out of their misery. And then? The baby's heart decelerates. Boom, C-section. Done in minutes. A miracle of modern science.

And just as the book predicted, I was induced, I labored for twelve hours, very little dilation, baby's heart rate decelerating. Time for a C-section. I was expecting it. I had not daydreamed fondly of childbirth. I was prepared to be wheeled into an OR. I had even discussed it with my sister, who is a gynecological oncologist, which means she performs high-risk surgeries several days a week. Listening to my sister talk about C-sections was like hearing an Olympic marathon runner describe a short walk. It bored her to even think about them.

Unfortunately, in my early twenties, I transcribed a talk by a world-renowned obstetrician that might be best summarized as "Things That Can Go Horribly Wrong During Childbirth, Quickly Killing the Mother While a World-Renowned Obstetrician Stands By Helplessly and Watches." So I mentioned a few key words to my sister, words like *streptococcus* and *toxic shock*. "These things are very rare," she said. I mentioned the movie *To Live*, set during the Cultural Revolution in China, in which two teenagers in an understaffed communist hospital try to deliver a baby and the mother bleeds out and dies. My sister blinked at me the way doctors sometimes do. "Those were fictional *teenagers*. In communist China. Decades ago." Right. I should probably just relax and trust medical science.

"But people do get these infections that kill them quickly," I said. "That still happens, for sure. And that seems pretty unpredictable!"

My sister didn't speak for a minute. She was weighing her options. "Just . . . make sure they examine the birth canal very closely, to make sure it's clean."

So that one item was on my to-do list: remind doctor to check birth canal, you know, to prevent immediate death. And what doctor doesn't love a little reminder from their patient, mid-surgery? *I trust medical science*, I said to myself again as two doctors rummaged around in my open belly like they were looking for something in a cabinet jam-packed with heavy sports equipment. Bill was standing up now and looking in the direction of my stomach. Then he sat down again and got very quiet.

"*Say something comforting*," I growled. Bill mumbled "Everything is fine," in a very Everything Is Not Fine I Just Saw Your Bloody Organs voice.

Then the doctors got very quiet in their rummaging, notably quiet, like maybe they'd broken some of the sports equipment and they'd misplaced some of it and maybe there was no football in here at all, the game was off, everyone should just go home. And just as I was starting to panic at how quiet they were: a cry.

High, piercing, like a tiny little cartoon-baby cry. *Waaaaa!*

Time stopped.

There was actually a baby in there! Not a puppy. Not a bowling ball. And the baby had a voice. The baby had a face and arms and legs. It was not an alien after all. It was a little baby girl.

You've seen this scene before. All I can tell you is that when you're the useless alien husk who created the baby, and you're pretty sure you might die and the baby might die and the hospital might burn down and really, it's starting to feel clear that all of these things *aren't* about to happen? Well, it's different. The doctors are suddenly laughing and saying the baby is healthy and they're stuffing all the sports equipment back into your cabinet and sewing you up and now the baby is all clean and wrapped up in a little blanket and has a tiny pink-striped hat on her round head and the baby isn't crying anymore, and the baby has blue-gray eyes that are huge and a face like an anime character and then the character blinks at you calmly like *Who are you? Are you my mother?*

It's different. The universe melts away like a candle in an oven.

Are you my mother? Blink, blink.

Tears rush out of my eyes. A waterfall of tears. I am a gutted fish, sliding out to sea on a tide of tears. *I am your mother.*

I look up at Bill and his face says, *See? I told you.* And that feels fine. Bill was right. He knew all along. We did it, the two of us. We made a person, and the person is here, and everything is beautiful.

∞

Babies look like one thing from a distance, and they look like a very different thing from close up. From a distance, babies are nuisances. They smell bad. They are loud. They create messes and work wherever they go. They present a never-ending string of inconveniences. Who would want that kind of a life? You'd have to be a masochist.

But once you get your own baby, you realize that babies are like Pokémon that change when exposed to different elements. One minute, your baby is a squishy pillow that loves to hug you; the next minute, your baby is a faintly grumpy gummy bear who mumbles and growls but is somehow wiser than you are. How is that possible? Then your baby is a soft woodland animal that smells like cedar chips and coos like a dove. *Aww.* But now something is wrong! Your baby screeches like a lemur when something is wrong!

Every day, you wake up to a new baby. Every few minutes, the baby changes. By the time you get your camera so you can take a picture of the growling gummy bear, it's already a lemur. But even when babies are wailing or enraged, it's strangely endearing. *This baby could bite my hand*, you say to yourself with a smile, pleased with your demonic little friend. *This baby might rip my hair out of my head with her grabby little fists!*

For the first few weeks I was home with the baby, all I did was watch the baby go from being a mouse to a cartoon pig to a beach ball to a pterodactyl. I felt a calm elation I had never experienced before. And since Bill knew all about babies, he saved me from freaking out around the clock the way most new mothers do. He said "Don't worry, she looks fine," or "That's just the way babies sound." He had a sense of humor about the baby, too. That part was crucial. He set the tone. He didn't panic. He found babies hilarious.

Bill took a whole month off just to hang around the house with me. When I was pregnant, it was astounding how much housework and cooking he'd sit back and let me handle, but now he did everything—cleaning and cooking and dealing with Zeke and my mom. When the baby got tired of nursing and needed to be burped or just walked around the house, Bill would jump in. He was the bouncer and the walker. My mom stayed for two weeks. My brother and sister-in-law, who lived two miles away from us in LA, had a baby the week before we did. When my mom wasn't at their house, she also cleaned and cooked and walked our baby around.

So while everyone else dealt with the house, my only job was to feed the baby, and also to be the baby's best friend in the universe. I was a big puffy raft, and she was my passenger. It was the best vacation I'd ever had. That was a big surprise: I was sure I'd have postpartum depression. I've always been a victim of bad hormones. Instead, I was lazing around in a fog, cheerful and relaxed and grateful to be alive. I don't know if I've ever been happier. In all of our photos of that time, I'm smiling.

I didn't expect to be that good with an infant. Instead, I melted into my role as adoring Madonna, witness, protector. Everything was serene and satisfying. It felt like a beginning but also an ending: here was something solid, at last. I must have done something right, to land here. I must have pleased the spirits of the dead. For the first time in my life, I understood what it meant to feel blessed.

$$\infty$$

The trouble didn't start until I had to leave the house.

I didn't *want* to leave the house at all. I wanted to be in the same room with the baby at all times. The baby slept next to our bed, next to me. I would wake up and watch her sleeping. I would make sure she was still breathing. That was my job. Sometimes it felt like I needed to will her to breathe. If I forgot to check, she might stop.

I wasn't the most worried new mother on the planet. I usually slept well. I took naps during the day. But handing the baby over to someone else felt scary, like I was making a big mistake. No one could be trusted. Bill could hold the baby if she got fussy, or if she needed a diaper change. My mom could hold the baby. I did need to shower sometimes. But I was the only one who could be trusted completely. I needed to know that Bill would be just as careful as I was being. I figured he should probably be *more* careful than me, just in case. I talked a lot about exactly how careful he should be.

"Relax," Bill started to say to me. "Just relax." The sound of those words made my pulse race. Who was *he* to tell me what was worth worrying about and what wasn't? Now that I knew a little more about babies, I was increasingly suspicious of just how relaxed Bill was about them.

After three weeks, I finally agreed to leave the house and meet a friend for lunch. It was strange to be out in the world without my baby. It felt wrong. I wondered what the baby was doing. What's she up to now, now, *now*? It almost felt like my body needed the baby, wanted the baby back. *Where is our baby?* my body wanted to know. *Did you mess up? Did you lose our baby?*

When I got home, I walked into the kitchen and there was Bill, holding the baby on one forearm—legs and arms dangling— while stirring steaming macaroni with the other hand. My baby was dangling over the pot, while Bill stirred and talked to Zeke. My baby was the size of a raw chicken. Bill had my chicken draped across his forearm. Her head was in his palm. Her limbs were hanging in the air. My chicken was hanging over a boiling pot.

I took a deep breath. "You've got to be kidding me."

"Just relax," Bill said.

"I can't leave the house if I find this happening when I return."

"Calm down," he said. A fatal mistake.

"Give me the baby."

"She's fine."

I got a little closer, so Bill could hear the murder in my voice. "Give. Me. The. Baby."

I took the baby and went to the bedroom and started to cry immediately. My mind was flooded with despairing thoughts. All alone, no one on my side. I could never leave the house again. I couldn't trust anyone else, ever. The baby would die if I left.

Bill came into the room. I could tell immediately that he was still in *Just Relax* mode.

Let me just interrupt to state the obvious for a second: this is the worst, most volatile combination of marital attitudes. When a defensive *Just Relax* energy meets a murderous *You Don't Get It* rage, you're in trouble. This was the main flavor of conflict Bill and I got into as newlyweds. But it was not good. Bill was very defensive when we met. Most men are pretty defensive, in my experience, possibly because I'm bossy and opinionated about everything, but Bill was a tiny bit worse than most. The irony of his *Just Relax* stance was that *he was not remotely relaxed when he said it.* He was often even angrier than I was, in my openly homicidal state.

Sadly, it took many years to notice that and adjust my approach accordingly. Even when I was the one with *cause* to be angry, even when I was the one bringing a problem to his attention, Bill would quickly become even angrier than I was, on the spot. Even when he knew he had done something wrong, he would immediately become more emotional and more pissed off than I was. In fact, the more wrong he was, the more defensive he seemed to be! How is *that* adaptive? *How did this mutant species of man not die off a long, long time ago?*

So just when I had touched down in a horrible, alienated land where I was sure I would never be able to leave the house again, Bill had arrived in a very different world of rage mixed with the certainty that I was completely nuts. And sadly, at dark and desperate times like these, Bill would dig up evidence of *other times* I had proven to be nuts. While I was hoping for an apology, Bill was forming his bulletproof presentation on Why You Are Unwell.

We were in a terrible place that day. But I also remember feeling, inside my bones, how high the stakes were in that moment. I could *not* be isolated with a baby and a defensive man who couldn't respect my wishes. I *had* to make this man understand me, at all costs.

So I slowed down. I promised Bill that I wouldn't yell, but I had something very important to explain to him, and he needed to listen without talking, for a long time. Because this was something that could break us. This was something that could destroy all of the trust and goodwill we shared. It was time for him to understand how much he would never understand about being a woman. And to his credit, he agreed to listen.

I told him that I had never felt so completely out of control of my fate before. I had never felt so vulnerable. The baby wasn't just a little friend we both cared about. The baby felt like a part of my body. It felt like I could only relax when the baby was in my arms. And when I gave him the baby and left the house, it felt like I was leaving my liver behind.

So when I came home, and I found him holding my liver over a pot of boiling water? And when he said "Relax"? That didn't *just* make me angry. It made me feel like I was about to die.

"I am a jumble of nerves," I told him. I was propped up on the bed, hair messy, eyes red, surrounded by a sea of crumpled tissues from crying and blowing my nose repeatedly. "Everything is so good, but I am raw. You have to understand. Being a woman is *different*. Carrying a baby around inside your body for almost a year is *different*. You just can't know what that's like. I need you to believe me on that front, trust it, suspend your disbelief."

Bill still looked angry. I took a deep breath and continued. "I was *wired* to create this separate being, and now that this being is outside my body, it's like my wires are all ripped up and exposed. Or maybe it's just that I've always been wired badly and I didn't know it until now. And look, it's all fine as long as she's *still right here next to me*. But when she's somewhere else, I feel like a house that's about to catch fire."

I remember saying that exact thing. A house on fire. I might've cycled through three or four metaphors for what I was feeling. It was a lot, but I needed for him to understand: You just don't know how it feels to live inside my skin at this moment, still recovering, still adjusting. Have some respect for that. *Relax* is an insult when your fucking house is on fire. *Relax* is a sharpened screwdriver to your temple.

This was when Bill told me he thought I was nuts. Not ideal, but thankfully, I kept taking deep breaths. I said, "You can call this crazy. Please. Call it whatever you want. I *feel* crazy, so go ahead. But you still need to *respect* these crazy feelings, if you want to stay married. You don't have to understand my feelings, you just have to operate as if you have the same feelings, for my sake."

Bill took this in. He did not reject this notion. But it was time to talk about math.

If you have the fortune (or misfortune!) of aligning yourself with a scientific mind, someone with a slight fixation on statistics and proof, you might find yourself in a conversation like this one. You're talking about emotions and suddenly he's talking about t-tests. Bill wanted to *inform* me that the things I worried about were unlikely: SIDS? Pretty unlikely after the first month. Being dropped into a pot of boiling water? He held Zeke like that for years, zero falls into boiling pots.

"And this thing about toddlers being run over by cars? You act like that happens all the time. It's lunacy. Why do I need this shit in my brain?"

His little stats lesson made me want to kick him in the shins, hard. Instead, I agreed that these things were pretty unlikely to happen. But I explained to him that when I said "Watch out!," I wasn't saying "Hey, this is very likely to happen, so be extra careful!" I was saying "Even if there is a one-in-a-million chance that we will run over the baby or leave the baby in the back seat of the car by accident, *I need you to consider it.* Because if it did happen, it would destroy you. It would destroy me. Our lives would essentially be over. The stakes are so high that it needs to be remembered. We need to be paranoid about these unlikely things because *we have control over them.* The stuff we can't control? We have to let go. But the stuff we have some control over? We have to keep inside our heads, even though it's taxing to do that."

"So I don't *just* want you to *tolerate my paranoia*, I want you to be paranoid too. I want your paranoia to match mine. When you hold that baby, which is like part of my body, I want you to feel the kind of fear that I feel. That will be the one thing that will make me relax. If you could try to match the vulnerable feeling I have now. If I saw you try to do that? That would help. Call it insane. But that's what I need."

I told him that I didn't want to turn against him. But if he juggled my liver like a clown and laughed at me when I was scared about it, he would make an enemy out of his closest ally.

Bill can be very defensive, but he does listen. If I'm not visibly pissed off, he'll let me speak for a long time, and he doesn't zone out or drift off (unless we're in bed and it's late, in which case my words are just the lullaby he needs to fall into a deep slumber). Bill tunes in to my metaphors, even if I'm mixing them together incoherently. He tries hard to understand the feelings I'm trying to express. If I try to communicate a feeling—and I throw in a lot of ideas around the feeling, which some people would find intolerable—Bill becomes more interested, not less.

I don't think that's a common trait, among men or even people in general. I don't think most people listen even *more* closely after ten minutes of a very emotional diatribe. As long as there is no blame implied, as long as I can describe reality without making it seem as if it's all Bill's fault, then he'll hear and he'll eventually get it. In this way, Bill taught me to describe my emotional landscape without implying any blame. And this conversation about the baby, just three weeks into our shared child-rearing experiment and two years into our relationship, was one of the best, most productive conversations we'd ever had.

Because I was desperate. When I saw that baby over that pot, I could see a path branching off the path we were on: I would cry and yell and ask for help, but Bill would laugh at me and do whatever he wanted instead. My marriage would mirror my childhood, with me trying to express my needs or emotions and my parents yelling and sending me to my room just for having needs and emotions. I wasn't going to live like that, not for very long. I'd rather be alone, and raise a kid alone, than live like that again.

Thankfully, Bill is Bill. He boarded a boat and sailed down my river of words until we reached dry land, together. It was exhausting. But by the end of our talk, he got it. He agreed to behave in ways that were guided by high stakes and my irrational feelings and to never say the words "Just relax" to a woman whose liver he was holding.

And after that, Bill rarely told me I was being hysterical when I described the toddlers who got left in the car or run over by a clueless grandparent backing out of the driveway. He even looked up the backing-out-of-the-driveway thing and said, "Jesus, this happens much more often than I thought!" He started to take on all of the low-odds possibilities until he was worrying about them himself. I formed Bill into a seismograph, in my image, because I knew I could only trust another seismograph.

And once I knew Bill was truly on my side and understood and would try hard not to be careless, I started to relax a little. I made a resolution to keep all of the looming threats in mind without losing sleep over the millions of ways a baby could die or become injured. Any time I went from safeguarding my kids to picturing something awful happening to them, I learned to stop myself.

I knew I would always be a Chicken Little, no matter what I

did. But once Bill got on board, we were Team Chicken Little. I didn't have to be alone in my worries and fears. And I could set some of them aside, trusting that it wasn't all up to me.

"Pretend the sky is falling with me," I told him, and he did. It was an act of love and solidarity. I was so grateful for it. It kept us glued together at a time when we could've fallen apart for good. I didn't have to hate myself for being a seismograph.

$$\infty$$

A baby is a marriage crisis. Someone might as well have stolen your car and driven it to Vegas with his new mistress. Someone might as well be smoking meth in the bathroom at night, and selling your nicest scarf on eBay to buy more meth.

The moment the baby arrives, your marriage is utterly different than it was before. Before, you were separate people. You only had to agree about which toothpaste to share, or to never share toothpaste. You only had to split up the housework, or just neglect it with no serious consequences. You didn't have to sync up your emotions. You didn't have to trust each other with your life.

Then the baby lands like a bomb in the middle of your life and lays waste to everything.

Bill had to follow my lead in ways he hadn't before, but I also had to let go of control if I was going to maintain my sanity and have a life outside our home. I had to find a way to see Bill as an equal, parenting-wise. I had to trust him. I had to pass him the baby and walk away.

After that conversation, I decided to trust him. I knew he could be absentminded. But when I walked out the door to run an errand or see a friend, I chose to trust that he could manage without me. I knew I had the necessary materials to become the worst sort of high-strung helicopter parent, and I wanted to make sure I didn't do that. But it required a leap of faith.

For all of the built-in oppressions of heterosexual relationships, there are times when it's helpful to say, "You have no way of understanding how this feels." "I am a nuclear reactor" is something I've said a lot since then. It's demeaning and sexist to put it that way, maybe, but it's also my reality: I'm enormously moody. There's no way around it. When I'm grumpy, I'm not just mildly annoyed. I am living in a world of chaos and clanging pots and my head is on fire. What I didn't realize, though, was that Bill is the same way. It took me over a decade to understand that.

And even though I knew my nature, it was hard to admit how vulnerable I felt. Because admitting that I felt out of control and fragile meant admitting that Bill had a lot of power, and I was dependent on him. Letting him in was hard.

We is not my favorite word, and it never has been. *We* means a family. As the youngest child in my family, *we* means "I get crushed by *you* and *you* and *you*." *We* have to decide together, as in a very slow-moving bureaucracy. *We* are in this together, and therefore my fate is tied to yours. *We* have to talk about this—in diplomatic tones, which sometimes feels too slow and inefficient, too frustrating. *We* might disagree, and then we will have to discuss it and even (gasp) compromise.

A baby arrives, and suddenly *we* are grappling with life-and-death stakes. All of that hand-wringing over the engagement, over the wedding? It looks like picking the proper scarf to wear while storming the beaches of Normandy. Everything has changed now.

Everything is up in the air. We might never get off this beach. The future is hazy. We are fighting for our lives now, together.

But when I looked at Bill, he was always on my side.

$$\infty$$

I loved to watch Bill pick up the baby and take her away for a diaper change. He would make a sputtering, roaring sound like a rocket taking off, and then she'd slowly blast straight up into the air. "Rocket maaaaaan, pushing out the poops up here alone." The baby would look over his shoulder, happy, as they left to get a new diaper. The baby was up for anything. The baby loved weird sounds and stupid songs—until she changed her mind and hated everything. So relatable, that baby.

Somehow, even when the whole world falls apart around you, the baby is still mystical, warm and soft, delightful and delighted. You can yell, and the baby is wise enough not to take it personally. You can cry, and the baby is merely curious why it is raining from your face. Somehow even though your marriage is in a kind of crisis now, you're sharing in the crisis together. You're laughing about the crisis.

Somehow, you'll manage it together. No one is in charge anymore, now you are two people looking at each other like "Oh god, what now?" It's like you *both* stole the car and drove it to Vegas with your mistress. It's like you're *both* secret criminals. You're both evil masterminds. You've *both* lost your doughnuts.

You agree, you agree, you agree. There is too much work to do. The baby weighs more than two bowling balls now. There are too many little bottles to heat up. There is nowhere to put the baby. There is too much juggling. There's not enough sleep.

It's good, though. *Really* good.

A baby is a cloud, a ball of white light, a sweet duckling that smells like vanilla beans, a giggling monster, an angry rabbit. A baby is a merciless lamb: fleecy, saucer-eyed, unforgiving, unrelenting, unstoppable.

"This baby is ruining our lives," I said to Bill.

"We live to serve," Bill said.

Pure joy. We're a family.

8

Meet Officer Cow

When the baby was three months old, I took her to a room where other babies were crying. I knew it would be hard. I was prepared. I handed her over. She started crying. Normally, she was a happy baby. Everyone told us that. So hearing her cry was jarring.

"She'll be fine once you leave," the girl said. She really was a girl, too, even though she had a master's in child development. This was the fancy baby place. We'd been paying for it for months, just to hold our spot. They made you pay at the beginning of the "school year," even if your baby wasn't old enough to start until halfway through the year. There were tall trees in the yard, and happy toddlers wandering across the grass, and people talked about feelings a lot. There was a developmental philosophy behind every choice the caregivers made. You did want a person with an advanced degree holding your baby while she cried, didn't you?

All eight of the babies in the small room were crying at once.

I didn't want to leave until they stopped. They never stopped. I didn't like the way the girl with the advanced degree was holding my baby. I didn't like the fact that she seemed a little depressed. I understood it, but I didn't like it. My baby was calm when she was at home. Now she was screeching.

They put my bottled milk in their fridge. In three hours I would have to pump again. They told me I could come back and pump upstairs, in their room for pumping, or I could nurse my baby myself, and they could wait and not feed her until I was back. Pump at home, pump there, nurse her there? The eight babies crying formed a wall of despair that I couldn't climb over. I wanted to leave, but I wanted to take my baby with me. I couldn't leave her there.

"I might . . ." Pump there or go home or nurse there or . . . I couldn't decide.

"Do whatever you want," the girl said with an edge to her voice. So I left. I got into my car and shut the door and cried for five minutes. Then I drove to a little coffee place nearby. I would drink coffee and write something and then in, let's see, two hours, I would drive back and pump or nurse the baby, in a room full of babies and girls with advanced degrees, very relaxing. I drank some coffee and tried to write some words. I thought about my baby, still crying, probably. *She's not crying,* I told myself. *They said she would stop soon. They always stop after you leave, they said.*

After two hours of not writing, I went back to check on the baby, and to pump. I walked in, and I heard a baby crying. It was *my* baby. I nursed her upstairs and then drove her home with me.

When I got home, I called Bill and told him I didn't like the day-care place. Master's degrees in child development did not magically prevent eight small babies from crying at the same time.

Everyone was very young in that room. Why were all of the young ones in one room together?

Bill warned me that he had a class in fifteen minutes, but he could talk until then.

I told him that the day-care place that we'd already invested a small fortune in was not very good at all, as it turned out. I was sure of this. It was obvious. The classrooms for older babies and toddlers looked great—the big easels for painting, the giant yard. I loved this place, it was the very best place, and if we bailed, then we would lose our spot. She would never make it to the enormous, grassy toddler yard, where small children ran wild and played in the mud and learned about nature from thoughtful professionals with advanced degrees.

Bill kept listening, as the clock ticked down before his first class of the year.

"Doesn't this feel like an important time in her life, developmentally?" I asked Bill, conjuring my own imaginary master's degree in child development. "Aren't babies' nervous systems and endocrine systems or whatever developing at this age, and doesn't undue stress place a strain on those systems?"

"I don't know," Bill said. This was a tell. The words "I don't know" almost never came out of his mouth. He was a tenured professor, which meant always pretending to know things and never admitting when he didn't know. I was starting to notice that nine times out of ten, his statements of fact, proclaimed in a tone of utter certainty, amounted to random guesses. I had taken to interrogating him aggressively when he claimed knowledge. Roughly half of the time, he'd crack on the witness stand. This particular "I don't know" was an act of diplomacy.

What he knew at that moment was that I was overwhelmed. We had been lolling around at home in a world of pure sunshine while we were both on leave, and now I had returned to my full-time staff job as a TV critic and the thirty hours a week of mandatory TV viewing that went along with it. Bill was back at work, commuting two hours a day minimum to his university across town, teaching classes, dealing with academic personnel issues—overlords and underlings that needed to be managed as diplomatically as he was managing me on that phone call. Bill could be impatient and reactive at home, but he was a very good manager. He never thought of his colleagues as overlords and underlings. That was *my* brutal perspective, cultivated while working from home, unfettered by hierarchies for over a decade.

"Everything you're saying makes sense. The baby rarely cries at home," Bill said, a slight uptick to his conversational pace as the sand in the hourglass ran low. "She's still very small. You tried this place out, and it's not working. I think we have to trust our instincts on this." Then he told me gently that he needed to go. I could hear students talking in the background. I felt a surge of panic. Now I was alone with the baby, and soon she'd wake up and it would all be up to me. My husband had more important things to do.

"I wish I could be there," Bill said. "But it's okay, honey. It's all going to be fine."

I chose to believe him. Because he didn't imply that I was foisting something onto him that wasn't really his problem, the way many of my exes had when I called them at work. One of my exes even had a rule that I wasn't allowed to call him during the day.

Bill never suggested that, as someone who drove across town most mornings and was surrounded by busy and important academic professionals, he couldn't possibly slow down to discuss what I, a strange neurotic dairy cow, had observed about the potential mood disorders at play in a member of the infant room staff at the wildly expensive day-care center that I myself had freely chosen. He also didn't say, "While we're on the subject of mood disorders . . ."

So I put down the phone and did some math. I've always found numbers comforting, even when they add up to "You can't possibly afford this." We could hire a nanny part-time for the same amount that we were paying for part-time care at that gorgeous paradise for small children. Our baby could hang out at home, and I could write there and nurse her whenever I wanted. I could pump in our bedroom, far away from a chorus of crying babies.

When Bill got home from work, I told him my plan. He congratulated me on finding a solution that would work for all of us.

∞

Through a friend, we found a nanny named Juana who was smart and funny and loved babies a lot. She actually listened to the baby. She could tell what the baby wanted. The baby loved Juana, too.

That part was a little challenging, to be honest. It was difficult to witness how happy the baby was to see Juana, and then hand the baby over to Juana, and then go into the dark bedroom to watch *Dexter* or *Real Housewives of New York* or whatever trivial or grim televisual entertainments I had to write about that week.

My work life had begun to seem very stupid. That's the strange thing about having a baby. Even when you intend to make the baby just one part of your rich and fulfilling life, babies are such miraculous beings that they make everything else look hopelessly dumb by comparison.

I wished I were a surgeon or a politician or a captain of industry. If I were a surgeon like my sister, I could give my baby to Juana in the morning and feel like a hero. If I had a heroic job, then Juana would be a hero for assisting me, and we could all feel like heroes together. Instead, I was a loser, which I proved by writing bad jokes about Real Housewife Ramona Singer's undying love for pinot grigio. The world was filled with people who did real, important jobs while I lazed around, pumping milk from my enormous breasts, and pondered whether Jill Zarin or Bethenny Frankel had the moral high ground in their latest squabble.

I loved having a baby around, and I loved sitting at the kitchen table, talking with Juana about her life in Guatemala and her teenage son and her other nanny jobs while the baby was sleeping. All of my other choices looked suspect. Sometimes I would call Bill at work and cry about what a pointless career I had, watching my third episode of *Jag* in a row while my baby frolicked happily with a much more grounded woman in the next room.

"You like having a job," Bill would remind me. "You're a writer. You won't be writing about TV forever. Try to enjoy it."

∞

One night when the baby was four months old, Bill needed to stay late at work. I hadn't been alone with the baby at night before. That fact alone made me feel like a spoiled loser. I was Ramona Singer, yelling "I need pinot grigio at all times," except replace white wine with my mom, my husband, and my nanny.

The baby was pure sunshine during the day, but she got grumpy at night. She could tell when you were bad at your job of making her less grumpy, too. She was used to a quality bounce, a precisely calibrated rocking motion. Bill and Juana and my mom had all sorts of walking and bouncing and talking routines that I, the dairy cow, wasn't familiar with. I had overspecialized.

All I had to do was whip out a boob, and it solved every problem. I would breastfeed her almost anywhere, free of shame. Once I sat in the middle of a crowded Italian restaurant, a rare night out with good friends, sipping a cold Italian beer with one hand while clutching a nursing baby under a blanket with the other. A sea of faces looked over at me nervously. It was an unusual choice, drinking a cold beer while nursing in public. But I had done my research: breasts are not placentas, nipples are not umbilical cords. Your body processes what you ingest (like, for example, beer) and then makes food from it (with only .0001 percent of a beer in it). These ignorant faces at the restaurant didn't know that. Let them stay ignorant! I didn't care! I wanted to drink one cold beer at a restaurant with my friends!

But that night alone with the baby, I was not sure of myself. I was afraid. First she cried a lot, more than usual. I had woken up before dawn that morning to work on my book. Then I wrote my TV column. Then I watched TV. (I recently found some to-do lists from this era, and I can't believe how much I was doing in a single day. Apparently whenever I wasn't feeding the baby, I was writing several pages, cleaning bathrooms, doing laundry, cooking. I'm much easier on myself now.)

The baby let me know that she was deeply dissatisfied with the customer service she was receiving. I did not put her to sleep the way she liked, and her face told me that she'd really like to speak to the manager. So I gave up and kept nursing her instead.

When she was falling asleep, I watched her face, to make sure she wasn't about to wake up. Infants' faces are strange when they're sleeping. Sometimes they look like they're seeing ghosts. They smile and roll their eyes, almost like they're much older than they are. But I didn't know that. Alone in the house that night, what I thought was, "My baby has an undiagnosed neurological disease. We've been ignoring the signs, but here they are, irrefutable, unmistakable. *This baby's brain is not functioning correctly!*"

As usual, it was my brain that was not functioning correctly. And as usual, I called Bill, crying. Bill was out to dinner with some colleagues, but he stepped outside to speak to me. I pictured him looking handsome and important in his suit, standing on some busy sidewalk in front of a nice restaurant in West LA. If only I were the one out to dinner, and he were the one at home.

"I think the baby has some type of brain problem!" I told him. I described what I was seeing. Bill laughed out loud. Then he apologized for laughing.

"That's just how babies look sometimes. They look like they're possessed."

"I am very bad at being alone with the baby," I said, starting to cry again.

"Honey. You're working too hard. Being alone with a baby is hard for everyone."

"Why am I so bad at this?"

"Everyone is bad at it sometimes."

"No. *I'm a shitty mother who watches TV all day and doesn't even know her own baby.*"

"That's not true. You're a good mother who knows her own limits and makes sure her baby is around people who care all day long. You have a good job and you're a great writer and you never wanted to be a stay-at-home mom. It's not wrong to have a job. You're doing fine."

I put down the phone. I went back to the bedroom, where the baby was sleeping in her co-sleeper. Her expressions looked funny to me then, and not strange. She was fine.

I call Bill too much, I thought. *I need to call him less.*

But I'd never had someone to call before. It had been years since I'd dated anyone who picked up the phone and said "Hey, honey," and sounded happy to hear from me, even though I was interrupting and surely I had a problem again and most definitely I would cry and probably even blame him for something.

I had never leaned on anyone who didn't mind being leaned on. My parents did a lot of things right, but they expected me to be tough and capable from a very young age. I wasn't supposed to cry about small things. I could ask for help and get it sometimes, but mostly I was expected to handle my problems by myself.

Bill seemed to enjoy feeling helpful, and never found my arguments that I was a total mess convincing. I had persuaded every boyfriend I'd ever had that I was pathetic. Bill never saw it. He looked at me, unshowered in soft pants, breaking out (thank god for his bad eyesight), complaining about the clogged drain or the army of dust bunnies under the bed, and he saw someone capable and smart. And it was true that I managed our money and paid our bills and I'd bought and fixed up our house by myself before he met me. He was seven years older than me, and he'd never saved a cent. But a weaker man would've just resented me for these differences. Instead, Bill reminded me of who I was, over and over again. He didn't see the lazy loser or the disgusting ghoul I saw. He saw someone who mostly had it together, who meant well, who was doing her best.

He told me I was too hard on myself. That's a tough thing for a spouse to do. Because when you have a son and a baby and two dogs and a house to deal with and you decide your spouse should be easier on herself, that means more work for you. We were both freaking out about how buried in work we were. I had never worked so hard in my life, every minute of the day. It felt like we were behind on everything—deadlines, laundry, bills, errands. The temptation to be a little too hard on ourselves and each other was constant. "Is this really how it should be?" I would ask myself, staring at the pile of laundry overflowing the hamper in the closet. "Is this how normal human adults live?" I would sometimes say, brushing a waft of dog hair off the couch just so I could sit down.

But Bill didn't want me to work harder. He looked at me and saw a hard worker, even when I was slacking off. He was the first person I'd ever known who told me to be good to myself, and acted like I deserved it. "You're already doing so much," he said repeatedly. It took so long to hear him.

$$\infty$$

When Claire was seven months old, we flew to Denver to visit Bill's entire family for the first time. Both of his parents had died years earlier, but he had seven siblings, and I hadn't met all of them yet.

It felt exciting to fly with the baby for the first time. It was even better to arrive at his brother Frank's house and drink a beer and eat some chips and salsa and chat while Claire bounced on my lap. All of Bill's siblings were gracious and had great senses of humor, which is the single most important thing when it comes to in-laws, if you ask me.

But traveling with a baby is unavoidably stressful. Caring for an unpredictable, throw-pillow-shaped blob around the clock does something to your nervous system, and it gets worse when other people are around, watching you do it. You become a strange combination of cow and cop. Maybe you let your baby breastfeed for a little too long, because she's always happy when she's doing it. Or she passes out, drunk on breast milk, and you lie there staring at her cute rabbit face for a few hours. You do this because you know that the second you move, she'll wake up and be cranky for the rest of the afternoon. You're in a new place, so who knows if she'll nap? If she doesn't nap, she'll get whiny and cry a lot, as babies do.

But when the first-time mother cow emerges from the basement room in her brother-in-law's house, she becomes Officer Cow. She puts the baby down on the rug and hovers as the baby crawls around looking for things to choke herself with. Then an aunt wants to pick the baby up and hold her in ways that are perhaps slightly ill-advised, maybe without supporting her head correctly, as Officer Cow lingers at her elbow, making worried noises. Please note that many of the aunts and uncles don't have kids of their own and don't seem entirely familiar with small babies. There are fourteen aunts and uncles in attendance and only three cousins present.

Sometimes an aunt holds the baby, and the baby gets a fearful look and then bursts into tears. Sometimes an uncle asks if the

baby can eat something absurd, like a fucking peanut. Officer Cow
shuts the fuck up about all of this, because she's not an idiot. Even
so, she is probably scowling a lot and she knows to keep watch at all
times. She has to, because Officer Cow's husband is neither cop nor
cow, plus he's getting drunk on the deck outside with his brothers
right now. (One of the brothers is strumming guitar not all that
rhythmically, which Officer Cow notices because Officer Cow is an
officer but *not* a gentleman.)

So Officer Cow spends a lot of her vacation—a vacation that
takes a ton of time and energy and costs real money that Officer Cow and her husband don't have at that moment—hovering
and worrying and even longing to be back in her basement room,
alone with the baby. Even though she is free to sip beer and chortle
along with the rest of the adults, Officer Cow's head is still filled
with questions like "Will the baby sleep in her porta-crib later or
cry all night, requiring us to start from zero with sleep training?"
and "Can I keep my hormonal cow/cop self from sobbing or yelling in this environment?" and "Who are these weird strangers I'm
chained to for life, anyway?"

Officer Cow is wired like a dirty bomb, in other words, one
with a piss-poor attitude.

The aunts and uncles recognize this, because they're not stupid. But they don't say a word about it. They're too nice for that.
That said, they don't have the best attitudes either, both because
this is their brother's second marriage (*Do we really have to do this
again?*) and because this second wife is not the most relaxed human
alive, by all appearances. Officer Cow seems high-strung and judgmental, and because the aunts and uncles in attendance are *also*
slightly high-strung and judgmental (in spite of the deceptively

chill beer-sipping and guitar-strumming), they recognize a dirty bomb when they see one. They don't love feeling judged. They don't love this outsider at their family reunion, if they're being honest. The baby is amazing, but Officer Cow? Not so much.

On the last day of our visit, the siblings collectively agree to take some group photos. Officer Cow is reminded of this by each and every one of her husband's siblings at least twice that day. "Photos are at four p.m.! *Don't be late!*" they tell her, over and over. Their reminders feel like a kind of condemnation: "We know you'll be in the basement with your baby all day, but don't miss this!" So Officer Cow builds her day around this plan, feeding the baby, putting makeup on her sleep-deprived cow face, brushing her pathetically tangled cow hair.

Officer Cow appears upstairs at exactly 4:00 p.m. Everyone looks showered and eager to begin. The first photograph is one with just Bill and his siblings, no spouses. The second photograph is of Bill and his siblings *plus* all of their children, but still no spouses. Officer Cow passes her baby to an aunt, feeling slightly odd about it, probably just because she's an exhausted mess.

The third photograph will include everyone present. But who will sit out? Another spouse valiantly volunteers!

Okay. Everyone is in place for the photo! Officer Cow holds her baby and smiles.

"Oh hey, you guys? Dan needs to leave for the airport right now, we've got to run!"

Everyone disperses *before* the photo is snapped. Officer Cow stands still, in disbelief, but her pulse begins to race and her face turns hot. *She was not in a single photograph.*

Suddenly, Officer Cow does not feel like a real part of these festivities at all. She is a subhuman half-person who conveniently gave birth to a member of this family, but she will never matter in the slightest. Her mind flashes back to how many times she heard her baby spoken of in a tone that seemed to erase her from the picture. Over and over again, the siblings seemed to be congratulating each other on how well *her* baby turned out. *Here is a true descendent of our clan,* they seemed to say. *Just look at what we made!* They said these things without looking at her or acknowledging her presence. It wasn't just her asshole imagination at work here. She suddenly realizes that she is just an inconvenient appendage at best. She could've stayed home, and no one would've minded at all.

"Fucking unreal," Officer Cow growls, and everyone hears her say it. She isn't sorry. She creeps back down to the basement, tears forming in her eyes, wishing that she could hop on the next plane out of town, too.

Officer Cow's husband comes downstairs after a few minutes. When he walks in, already studying her face, she knows he understands. She doesn't have to explain. "That was crazy," he says to her. "They're fucking crazy."

Officer Cow puts her head on her husband's shoulder. Tears roll down her face, onto the sleeping baby. "It's fine. Families are weird. I get it."

$$\infty$$

Having a baby means becoming a new kind of person you don't recognize. Even though I knew that, and dreaded it, and tried to prepare for it, there was no real way to anticipate how radically my life and my self-image were going to change.

And really, the hard work had just begun. Bill's patience with me would eventually be tested. But that first year with Zeke and the baby, I always knew how lucky I was. Bill reminded me so many times that I was doing fine, that we were doing fine. I counted on him to keep me steady. I would start to lose my grip and start talking in circles and Bill would listen. I had never had a friend like that before. It changed everything.

And when the baby started at a different day care run by a Presbyterian church three days a week, one staffed by older women who didn't have any advanced degrees and gave curt instructions to toddlers who barely understood language yet, Bill laughed instead of worrying about it. We would pick the baby up from a room filled with plastic toys or pluck her from a giant ugly cement yard. She would be wheeling around in a big car or she would be sitting nicely at a plastic table with other babies, eating a Ritz cracker with gusto because she had only been eating apples and spinach and milk up to then, not flour and sugar and salt pressed into a buttery disk. One day when Bill arrived, she and the other toddlers were eating powdered doughnuts. Bill stopped by the day-care director's office to let her know that Jesus himself wouldn't feed a one-year-old kid powdered doughnuts as a snack.

Even so, we tried very hard to relax our standards that year. We reminded each other of what probably mattered and what maybe didn't. Our lives had become a rolling crisis management meeting, demanding a constant reshuffling of priorities. But we managed it all, mostly without falling apart.

To reward ourselves for how hard we were working, we'd pick Claire up from day care some days and drive to the Mexican restaurant that we loved nearby, the one we really couldn't afford because we weren't making much money and we were spending so much of it on day care. We'd order margaritas and talk while the baby smeared black beans all over her face.

It was so rare to actually be looking into each other's eyes that year. Our lives of lolling around in bed had segued into a filthy hurricane of baby, stepson, dogs, groceries, dirty dishes, and dirty diapers. But those nights at our favorite restaurant, we were in the eye of the storm. We could look up at the small circle of blue sky and remember how it felt to relax, to take in the moment, to appreciate what we had. We were at the center, and everything was good. We were in love.

9

Aging Viciously

When the baby is about a year old, Bill and I leave her with a babysitter in order to attend the wedding of a close friend. I am sipping a cocktail before the ceremony when a man with a head like a grouper observes that I look completely different now that I've had a kid. He fixes me with one fish eye stuck in the side of his head like a Picasso painting and tells me that just a few years earlier, when we both used to hang out with our mutual friend, the bride, I had been very hot indeed, but now? Utterly unremarkable. "You gained weight, sure, but that's not all," he gurgles. "Your *face* isn't the same. Like I didn't even *recognize* you." His gills hiss and spit out seawater as he laughs, spattering my dress with little bits of seaweed and foam from the tides.

For the first time in my life, I don't have a laugh and a swift counterattack at my disposal. I look for my usual defense mechanisms, and they aren't there. Maybe my verbal left jab dried up and tumbled away like my tangled mess of straw hair was poised to do. Maybe my wit seeped out of my body with the blood of childbirth, or maybe it got absorbed into the flab of my face, which I suddenly realize is just a giant, featureless ass cheek. Maybe my charms are hidden in the infinite folds of what I now recognize as a misshapen, bloated body. It's as if someone found a whale's corpse rotting on the sand and tried to stuff it into a cute little cocktail dress.

Sure, I knew I'd gained a few pounds and my hair had turned frizzy after I stopped breastfeeding, but I'd still been feeling pretty good about myself. Now I'm living that nightmare where you're in class and you look down and you're not wearing any pants. The worst part of the dream isn't that your bare butt feels all wrong on the wooden chair. It's that everyone else knew all along. You were the last one to notice. You kept cluelessly acting like your usual self.

Feeling hideous, I sit down with Bill and my friends and wait for the wedding to begin. A man with the face of an angry raccoon walks up to the pulpit, another friend of the bride I've met a few times over the years. He's been ordained by the Universal Life Church so he can perform the ceremony, which he lets us know as he scratches furiously behind one of his pointy ears with a gnarled claw. He tells us the bride is running late, typical of her, nothing to worry about, and then he makes a joke about how she's probably getting cold feet. The crowd titters unappreciatively, but the angry animal's bloodshot eyes narrow as he laps up his drink greedily, using both of his little raccoon hands. Then he digs in deeper.

Once he's worked through all of his prepared material, along with several strong drinks, he resorts to heckling the wedding guests. He doesn't get to me until right before the bride enters. He's mentioned a few times by then that the bride is lovely and perfect and her husband isn't good enough for her, which is probably why the crowd has gone completely silent, save for a gaggle of the bride's most supportive friends, who are exchanging weary glances while doing their best imitation of a raucous laugh track, trying to signal that everything is fine, this is just a normal wedding, it's all in good fun. I'm one of the ones laughing, a big, soft, stupid mom with a twisted head of flammable straw where her hair should go, trying to save the moment, trying to spackle over the awkwardness and turn this extra-dark episode of *The Office* back into the dreamy wedding that my friend wants it to be.

Unfortunately, when you show an angry little raccoon with shit stuck in its butt hair that you can take a joke, sometimes you're also showing him that you can take anything—a private excoriation, a public beatdown, an endless trickle of negs, a quiet, continuous undermining, a slow erosion of your confidence, a sudden jolt to your system strong enough to make all of your illusions cave in on themselves.

So the raccoon turns to the crowd and, with a weighty look that says *Now this part is serious*, explains that because the bride has settled for less than she deserves, soon she'll end up just like me, unrecognizable from before. (Apparently the grouper and the raccoon had a fun little chat and exchanged some notes before the ceremony.) Then he takes a minute to explain that just a short time ago, I was exceptional, gorgeous, unnervingly so. He waves his little claws in the air as if to say *Wow, the power of that!* But now? What happened? Who is this? "Once she was Mary Tyler Moore, and now . . . she's Rhoda."

I smile, lips closed. *Rhoda is hot*, my mind weakly offers. Bill looks at me with wide eyes like I might set something on fire. Later, he tells me he wanted to walk up to the front of the room and beat the man to a bloody pulp in front of everyone, but he didn't want to make a scene, for the sake of our friend.

But that's what happens anyway. The bride enters, but unbelievably enough, the comedy routine keeps going and everything gets even darker and more awkward until you can feel the whole room full of guests telepathically agreeing to walk straight into the ocean together.

Afterward in the bathroom, the bride asks me if the wedding ceremony was really okay or if it was a complete disastrous nightmare like it very much seemed to be the vast majority of the time. As I draw random black lines around my hideous ass-cheek face to emphasize the tiny bug eyes that are hiding behind mountains of flesh, I tell her the ceremony was extra super funny and great and fuck anyone who can't take a joke.

And so we tumble back out into the hallway, back to the vicious rabble chain-smoking on the stairs, back to the circles of dumbstruck relatives biting their tongues as the clock ticks down. We sink back into a lifetime of inviting jokes shaped like fuck-yous, jokes that show exactly how a petty woodland varmint or a man-sized grouper can want you desperately while resenting and hating you for it, jokes that lay bare the core belief that no woman should have power for very long, jokes that suggest that when a man rips that power out of a woman's hands, that man is a hero.

But I'm already old enough to know that the world is filthy

with scrabbling predators and slow-moving bottom feeders who'll fluff me up only to cheer my rapid demise. It's happened before. What feels certain that night is that even if I get my swift verbal right hook back, my jabs won't land anymore. Only a hot girl can hurt your feelings. Everyone else is execrable.

As Bill and I drive home from the wedding, I think about how anxious those men were to let me know that I'd lost my power and standing in the world, just by signing up to one man in particular who wasn't them. That's what they were telling the bride, too: This wedding is your funeral. This is the death of your magic. Soon you won't be special anymore. You're making a big mistake.

Rarely do these messages come through quite so clearly and brutally. But women encounter smaller, more subtle replicas of the same message everywhere. Getting married and having a kid shifts your entire understanding of yourself as a woman. How could it not? A lot of people treat you as if your charms are lost and gone forever. What I grew to hate the most, though, was how the women around me echoed those messages to themselves and each other, as if the only feminine and lovable and natural thing to do was to fade ever so gently into the background and pour all of your energy into your husband and children.

I didn't want to live that way. When I heard women on reality TV shows saying things like "I'm just a mom, showing all the moms that they can do anything!" it made my skin crawl. When I'd go out with mom friends, I'd hear the same thing from the men around us: "Just a bunch of moms cutting loose, huh?" one guy said at a bar when he spotted us. How had I gone from being a woman to being some asexual blob that's dragging her ghost children with her everywhere she goes? Why wasn't I allowed to live inside a delusional bubble that told me I hadn't changed a bit, the way most men did when they left the house?

Everyone seemed to agree with the same defeated narrative. When I insisted that I was still the same obnoxious weirdo I'd always been, and I still wanted to have fun and I still craved attention sometimes, people sometimes acted like that was tacky of me. Even my close friends seemed to hint that it was a little greedy, to get the husband and the kid and *still* want more.

But not Bill. On our way home, Bill tells me that I am just as attractive as ever and those two guys are just sad little assholes yanking at their flaccid dicks at night, alone and furious. He tells me that most of all, he feels bad for the bride, a smart, lovable woman who has surrounded herself with contemptuous brutes because they give her the exact diet of praise and mocking that feels like home to her.

"That sounds like me," I say.

"Not anymore," he says.

"I'm gross," I say.

"Not to me," he says.

I still walk around feeling like an overstuffed armchair for months after that. I don't diet constantly or obsess about my Gilda Radner hair enough to fix it, but when I look in the mirror I feel embarrassed for myself all over again.

But I know that it's selfish and vain to make an effort. As a mother, I'm supposed to have matured beyond vanity. I'm supposed to accept my new supporting role in life, fading sweetly and softly into the background so that all of the men and *some* of the women—the young ones and the slightly older ones who've stayed effortlessly hot—can have their good times without a rotund, inconvenient *mom obstacle* getting in their way.

It's better this way, I tell myself. *I've changed. I've evolved beyond vanity.* Trying way too hard means you're pathetic and unlovable. Giving up on looking good means you're wise and strong and a good mother.

Looking back years later, though, I realize that I sacrificed way too much, just to take the proper, humble, maternal shape that was expected of me. I felt invisible for years, and I thought that was just how it had to be. I pretended it was fine. I lied straight to people's faces, day in and day out, about the strength of my desire for more. In order to be a married woman and a mother, in order to age gracefully, I had to prove that I could take anything: a private excoriation, a public beatdown, an endless trickle of negs, a quiet, continuous undermining, a slow erosion of my confidence, a sudden jolt to my system strong enough to make all of my illusions cave in on themselves. I would eat it and smile through closed lips. I would pretend I didn't hear a word, didn't see a thing, was utterly in the dark, a gorgeous, silent vessel still built to hold the most merciless man's limited imagination.

Now that I was married and had a baby, I wasn't meant to cluelessly keep acting like my usual self. Instead, I should start pretending that my power was running out, like a battery losing its charge. I should always be fine with whatever happens. *It's better this way.* I had to live in reality, to make more room for fishy heads to spray and claws to wave in the air, to let go, to give up. Otherwise I was just a sick, greedy whore who was trying desperately to be young again—and mostly failing dramatically.

Bill had no tolerance for this story. He kept telling me that I could be as big and bright as I wanted to be. He never said I was vain. He encouraged me to take whatever I needed without apologizing for it.

And eventually, I would get even greedier. That's the paradox of feeling safe, feeling secure, for the first time in your life. It offers you the luxury of wanting even more, sometimes to your own detriment.

10

Vertigo

I worry about the state of your marriage."

These aren't words you want to hear out of anyone's mouth, least of all your mother's. But this is how it works with marriage and kids. First you abandon your dignity to merge with another flawed human, and then you start making miniature flawed humans, and then life knocks you down and grinds you into the sand, and just when you think you're going to make it?

That's when your mother shows up. And your mother does not think you'll make it. She thinks you're screwed.

We had been planning to visit Travel Town, a train museum in Griffith Park, so our older daughter, Claire, age two and a half, could have a little fun. She hadn't had much fun for a long time, thanks to the arrival of her baby sister, Ivy, two weeks prior. But we weren't that good at leaving the house with two kids yet. I had been getting so little sleep that I was exhausted to the point of feeling sick. It felt laborious just to pack the diaper bag. And the truth was, the whole trip was mostly an attempt to convince my mother that we were still functioning as a family.

My mom had been staying with us for a full week by then, so she already knew we were struggling. The serene wonderment of my previous postpartum experience had been replaced by a cyclone of terse commands, grime, and raw panic. When people say two kids are easier than one, they're talking about a five-year-old and a seven-year-old. They're not talking about a newborn and a toddler. For the first six months you have a newborn and a toddler, you're in a deep, dark tunnel under the ocean.

Someone in the house is always holding the baby while sweeping while someone else is talking to the toddler while herding the dogs and paying a bill. Someone is vacuuming and yelling while someone else is breastfeeding and crying. Someone asks, "Can you handle this?" and someone else yells, "I'm *doing something* right now!" The structure of our world had tipped sideways and tumbled to the ground, like those wobbly structures in the old Angry Birds game everyone used to play a decade ago.

Bill stands and watches me while I pack the 7,402 items we'll require just to leave the house. He is telling me where I should and shouldn't place various items. He sees himself as the boss of the diaper bag. But I'm so tired that the noise coming out of his face sounds warped and scoldy, like the incomprehensible *waa-waa-waaa* of teachers in Charlie Brown TV specials. In the background, a nerve-rattling ambient jumble of babbling toddler and grumbling mom and the nervous clicking of little dog claws on the floor continues. The dogs are anxious that we're leaving the house without them. I'm anxious that I have to go on this excursion at all. I want to stay at home like Jabba the Hutt, eating frogs and napping with my eyes half open. But I can't afford to let my mom believe that I'd pass up a chance to have some outdoor fun with my toddler. I need to look like A Good Mother. I need to do Good Mother shit somewhere my mother can watch me do it.

We are hurling ourselves at the wreckage, in other words. I can feel my pulse skyrocket. My nervous system is the trampoline that takes every bit of emotion hurled its way and launches it in some other direction, like a bomb.

"No, I just *said* . . . ," Bill is correcting me again. I can feel my teeth clench. "Let me do this *the way I fucking do it*," I hiss. He is not picking up on the distinct note of homicide in my tone. He presses his point angrily. There is *one* proper way to make everything fit! My hissing rises a decibel. My mother scowls and leaves the room. The dogs stop pacing and look at us with fear in their eyes. The baby starts making those sputtering sounds that babies make when the atmosphere shifts in ways that displease them. Their nervous systems are trampolines, too.

We make it to the car and we are all packed in, the whole family. But when I try to put my key in the ignition, I feel too sick to drive. I stop and close my eyes. *Do not yell. Your mom already thinks you're losing it. She's already unnerved by what a mess you are.*

Unfortunately, *Do Not Yell, Your Disapproving Mother Is Watching* is a recipe for total system collapse on my planet.

"You know what? I need everyone in this car to listen to me right now. Listen! Are you listening? I AM THE ONE IN THIS CAR WHO DOES NOT FUCKING SLEEP. ME. *I'M* THE ONE. Do you know how many hours of sleep I got last night? Three. Three *fucking hours*. The night before that? Two hours. The night before? Four hours. INCREDIBLE. Do you know how that feels?

Nine hours of sleep over the course of three days? Can you imagine? NO, you *cannot* imagine. *BECAUSE I AM THE ONE. I AM THE ONLY FUCKING ONE HERE WHO KNOWS.* SO PLEASE. DO NOT EVEN FUCKING DREAM OF GIVING ME A HARD TIME RIGHT NOW. IT WILL NOT GO WELL. BECAUSE I *AM FUCKING LOSING IT, OKAY?* I AM FUCKED RIGHT NOW! I AM TOTALLY FUCKING *FUCKED!*"

I burst into tears. I look into the rearview mirror and see that Claire is very worried. My mom is grimacing and blinking, an act of tremendous restraint. Her face indicates that I will pay for this, sooner or later.

And the baby is . . . incredibly enough, asleep. Babies are survivors. They will take their sleep as needed. They do not care how fucked you are right now.

I turn and look at Bill. His anger has evaporated completely. You can see in his placid face a reflection of his adaptive genes, the genes of conquistadors and cliff dwellers who could sense danger in their nerves long before it crept into the village on predatory feet or clamored in on a warhorse. This man knows a true calamity when he sees one. This man is a survivor.

Bill is my only friend. He puts a tentative hand on my knee.

It's a whole new thing, to have a partner who loves you even after the wheels come off. In my family, you yelled, and even though you were just speaking the goddamn lingua franca of your native habitat, you were banished to your room for it—all alone, for hours. Your lack of control was shameful. Somehow it made everyone else look bad. Your yelling proved that *you* were the problem. Oddly enough, *their* yelling *also* proved that you were the problem.

But Bill looks at me with eyes that say, *You are not the problem.*

Even though my voice was just saying, *I will rip your face apart with my bare hands if you don't let me sleep,* his eyes are saying, *This system collapse makes perfect sense.*

And he's right. Right now we have a baby, a toddler, a preteen, a mother, and two very bad dogs, all living in a tiny house together, a house coated in filth and dog hair. We both have full-time jobs. The dogs need to walk every single day, or they'll bounce off the walls and rip little socks and toys and diapers to shreds. Claire goes to an acceptably mediocre day care, and soon the baby will have a part-time nanny who will turn out to be truly terrible with babies.

"I feel like I'm hallucinating right now," I tell Bill. "My vision is clear and weird and I have a pounding headache, like I'm on drugs."

"I sorry, Mommy!" Claire is crying now.

"It's okay, Claire. It's not your fault. Mommy is just so tired. Being tired makes you mad for no reason. That giant baby wants to eat constantly. But it has nothing to do with you. I'm sorry for yelling!"

"It's fine," Bill says, clearly for my mother's benefit. "This is just where we are. I need to remember how little sleep you're getting." We are having a family therapy session in my car, but my mom is not speaking. She is not agreeing that it's fine.

"I'm really sorry," I say again.

"Do you want me to drive?" Bill says.

"No, it's okay, I can do this."

"Maybe we should try to make sure you take a nap when we get back."

"Okay. Thanks, honey. I love you."

∞

We are halfway to Travel Town when my mom finally says it: "I worry about the state of your marriage." Her announcement comes out of the blue. We are listening to music. Everyone is relaxed. Everyone has moved on.

My mom keeps talking. "Of course you don't *believe* your marriage is in trouble. Couples *always* think things are fine, and then, boom, one of them is just done. You never know until it happens!"

"You really don't need to worry about our marriage," Bill tells her. "We're just not sleeping."

"Oh, believe me, I know that every couple has their little squabbles," my mom says, and I can feel myself relax a little. "But those fights add up. And sometimes men don't realize how much that kind of bickering bothers them until they're already out the door."

This might be a good time to tell you that I love my mother. She's a brilliant, capable, generous human being who taught me how to ride a bike, bake bread, play solitaire, and defend myself verbally against anyone under the sun. My mom read to me every night when I was little. Together, we baked cookies and played board games and painted on canvases on the back patio. And after my mom and dad got divorced, life with my mom often felt like a party. She'd put on Diana Ross's "Upside Down" and dance around the living room like a disco queen. She let us adopt a second rescue dog, and then she packed three kids and two dogs and a tent into her tiny yellow Le Car and drove us straight to Myrtle Beach to camp out in the sand, just so we got out of the house without spending money we didn't have. My mom was wise and funny and she talked to me like I was smart from a very young age.

My mom is the reason I always wanted to have kids. She made being a parent look fun. She felt strongly that you shouldn't over-think these things, you just had to go for it. Instead of worrying if you could handle big life events, you just dove in. You had to work hard, sure, but most of all you had to be optimistic about what came next. For years as a single mom, she was very stressed out and very broke. But she never sounded envious or contemptuous. She worked hard to maintain her optimism. Even when we were subsisting below the poverty line, my mom didn't want her three kids to grow up around someone who seemed defeated or unhappy or angry at the world. She wanted us to understand that joy was possible, that we should believe in joy. She didn't put that senti-ment into words very often, but that wasn't what mattered. What mattered was that she *embodied* joy.

That said, one thing that's, um, slightly *unusual* about my mom is that when *you* are embodying joy, just like she taught you to do, she sometimes gets a little grumpy.

Weird, right? Remember my wedding? That's one obvious ex-ample, but there are so many others. Like if you say, "Mom, I want to take you to the best restaurant in town. You will not believe how good it is!" you can absolutely guarantee that my mom will politely thank you for inviting her, quietly eat everything on her plate, and then, at the end of the meal, declare the experience disappointing and not remotely worth the money. When you gush, my mom ei-ther silently cringes or debates you.

Or, if you say to my mom, "Hey, I found this really cool board game! You're gonna love it!" she'll play the board game with a slightly pinched look on her face, but she'll say nothing, and then, at the end of the game, she'll tell you that your new game is really not that great. No big deal, but nope. Not a fun game. Who could like a game like that? No one.

Once, early in my marriage, at a time when I would often tell my mother how helpful and kind Bill was, my mom finally snapped. "Oh, Bill, Bill, *Bill*," she said, sounding disgusted. "He's not so perfect, you know!" (Now I like to say this to Bill any time he's feeling unusually proud of himself.)

So even though my mom taught me to be capable and resilient and optimistic, when I bounce back from a setback and I seem a tiny bit smug about it, that makes my mother a little hostile. Her answer to "I am happy!" or "This tastes delicious!" or "Wow, what a day!" is the same: *I'll be the judge of that.*

But it's also understandable that her adult daughter's wild emotional roller coasters would get under her skin. The children of alcoholics are not known for their love of other people's unpredictable emotions, for obvious reasons. And when my mom is under stress, she stops making sense. Plus, my freak-outs feel personal to her. They mean I'm fucking up my life. There's nothing she can do about it, but it's all her fault.

It's funny how we create our own crucibles for ourselves. First my mother has a very sensitive, moody daughter who talks about her emotions constantly, and then I drag my mom straight into my volatile life in the wake of having a second baby, expecting her to tolerate the unprecedented level of chaos that's unfolding around us.

My mother's best solution to emotional stress is to move straight to the worst-case scenario. Might as well discuss divorce right up front, since it's clearly just a matter of time!

"Susan, I understand what you're saying, but I'm fine," Bill tells my mom. "I'm not going anywhere."

"That's what you think now. Things change before you realize it."

"My mind doesn't even go there."

"Not *yet*, anyway. But there's only so much stress one person can take."

"Well, I guess we'd better enjoy this marriage while it lasts, then," Bill says, looking at me and smiling, "since it'll be over before either of us know it."

"That's not what I'm saying," my mom says.

"You're so sure that *Bill* will dump *me*," I say. "What if I dump him first?"

"Heather. Anything can happen. This isn't about Bill." There is a pause. "Although men often don't know what they're feeling until it's too late."

Marriage is a spectacle, and everyone is invited to watch. But no matter what my mom says, my marriage doesn't feel fragile. Everything else might be breaking down, but Bill and I feel solid, maybe more solid than we ever have before. We're so solid that I almost don't care who can tell. All that matters is that Bill and I can.

When we arrive at Travel Town, I apologize to Claire again, but she seems to have forgotten the whole thing. Nothing unusual has happened, as far as she's concerned. Your house is just like your acceptably mediocre day care: everyone yells at each other, and then you get to eat powdered sugar–covered doughnuts that come out of a huge bag, and then everyone is happy and has sugar all over their faces. The world is not really collapsing. These birds are not that angry, that's just the natural shape their faces make.

Later that night in our bedroom, Bill and I joke about my

mom's skepticism. It seems ludicrous that she can't pick up on our trust in each other, can't sense that we're in this together and no one is going anywhere. It's hard to understand how she can have such a suspicious read on us. Our home is nestled in the side of a cliff, safe from invaders. This cliff is not crumbling. We're safe.

$$\infty$$

The circle of blue sky above our heads is closing up nonetheless. My hallucinatory lack of sleep segues into a string of illnesses. First I have a horrible form of dysentery that sends me stumbling to the bathroom in the middle of the night. I pass out and crack my rib against the side of the bathtub, which I have mistaken for the toilet. Bill discovers me in a crumpled heap and spends the next half hour cleaning me up while I am barely conscious, sweating, and confused. Next, I get the flu but I'm afraid to take any medicine because I'm breastfeeding, so I lie in bed crying and begging for more soup, more Gatorade, more ice water. Bill is a pale ghost, carrying the baby around in circles and talking to the toddler and bringing me liquids and running to the store with both children.

He returns from the store, and I ask why it took so long. He says it fucking took so long because Claire started yelling and the baby started crying and he had to change a fucking diaper in the grocery store bathroom and they didn't have a fucking changing table so he had to do it on the cement floor. *So yeah. It took a while.*

"I know it sucks. I know," I say. "But honestly, I'm worried, because I feel like I'm dying."

"Well, you're *not* dying."

"I *feel* like I am. That's all I'm saying. I'm just telling you how it feels."

This is when Bill breaks and starts yelling. He doesn't care if I feel like I'm a fucking dragon sprouting wings and flying into the sun. He has shit to do. "Tell me what you want," he says. "Just tell me what you need. I have to go deal. Keep in mind that I am fucking dealing with everything."

"You hate weakness," I say. "You think weakness is gross."

"No! I'm just *busy*, okay?"

Bill leaves. I sob. Now I feel like I'm dying and I'm being rejected at the same time. Maybe this is a feature of that rock-bottom feeling you sometimes get when you're married: All bad emotions come packaged with other bad emotions. No sadness is just sadness. No weakness is just weakness. Sadness is desperation is shame is weakness is grief is desolation is longing is abandonment is death.

One week later Bill gets the flu, too. I bring him a steady flow of beverages and soups and smoothies. I fetch him medicines. I urge him to drink more Gatorade. I am a dream nurse, and I am grinding my dreaminess into his face: *See. This is how you do it, motherfucker.* I also take the kids to the park and clean the entire house. I don't feel like I'm dying anymore. I feel like I've been saved from the brink of death, and now I'm thrilled and grateful just to be alive.

I'm also gloating. *I am so much hardier than you,* I think as I make Bill tea and soup and the kids sleep and the dogs nap. The kitchen floor is clean. The dishes are done. I got up early and fixed everything, *as always.*

I float into the stinky room where Bill is coughing and crusty and miserable, and set down the tea and the soup.

"I get it now," he says. "I feel like I'm dying. I'm pretty sure that I'm dying, in fact."

"Yep."

"I'm sorry. I feel like such an asshole."

"You hate weakness," I say.

"It's true. I don't like weakness. It's all I can think about right now. I feel so guilty about it."

Bill does sometimes learn things. And when he learns something from me, it's pretty satisfying. Because at first, he's stubborn about it. He doesn't want to give me credit for it. He wants to pretend it happened magically. This was a satisfyingly rapid about-face. I appreciated the assist from God, striking Bill down for his arrogance . . . you know, his arrogant cooking and shopping and his arrogant diaper-changing.

Bill never got angry at me when I was sick again. And that was helpful, because a few months later I came down with a fever and it turned out that I had pneumonia, and that was also when I discovered I'd cracked my rib when I was violently ill, which was why my coughing hurt so much. It felt like I was dying for a pretty good reason.

And just as the pneumonia was finally under control, I had to stay up very late to write a recap of the final episode of *Lost*, and when I woke up three hours later, the room was spinning violently and I couldn't walk. I called Bill on his way to driving Zeke to school across town. "I don't think I can pick up the baby right now," I said.

Bill drove back to the house. I was on the floor of the baby's room, which was also the laundry room, trying to stop the world from spinning. The baby was crying. Claire wasn't up yet. Bill took over, and I went back to bed.

The room kept spinning for three days. I should've gone to the doctor immediately, but I'd looked it up and it seemed like there was nothing they could do to help me. Once I finally made it to a doctor, they said the drugs wouldn't help anymore because you have to take them right after the vertigo starts. They gave me a bunch of strange exercises instead, to teach my brain how to process the information it was receiving, so that it could tell, literally, which way was up. I spent several minutes every hour staring at a point on the ceiling while falling sideways onto a bed. I felt like a crazy person but I kept doing it anyway.

After three more days, the spinning became more like seasickness. Three weeks later, it was my birthday, so we had some friends over to the house. I sat in the corner, miserable. My head felt like a boat on the open ocean.

A month after that, the boat hit calmer seas. I started to go on long walks and then runs again. I started to focus on sleep. I could sleep for ten hours at a time. I could nap for three hours. It was like I was making up for lost sleep, every day. I can't remember having a lot of complicated feelings about the world at that point. I was just trying to get my footing. The storm hadn't lifted for months. Our lives were pure chaos. This was about survival.

∞

At the end of June, Bill flew to Switzerland for a week, and I was alone with both kids. The baby was three months old and Claire was almost three. My capable, overachieving self kicked into high gear. We had purchased a jogging stroller and rarely used it. But I knew that if I spent a full week without Bill, I was going to need to get a lot of exercise just to stay sane. The dogs would need it, too. If I was going to leave the house, I'd have to do it first thing, too. If an activity didn't happen before noon, it would never happen.

First I loaded the double jogging stroller into the hatchback. Then the dogs sat on top, each one tied to the handles inside the back of the car, so they couldn't jump on top of the baby. Then the baby and the toddler and the diaper bag with books and snacks got packed into the back seat. The baby was always crying by the time we got into the car. This made the dogs nervous: *Can't someone fix that thing and make it shut up?* Claire talked a steady stream, or sang, or talked and sang and talked and sang. Her approach to the baby was: *I do not see you. Your noises mean nothing to me.* When we arrived at the trail that circles around the Rose Bowl, I took the stroller out and set it up. The dogs whined. The baby screamed. Claire asked, "Mommy, Mommy, can I get out? Mommy, get me out!"

I packed the kids into the jogging stroller, side by side. I gave Claire her snacks. I gave Ivy her bottle. I put board books next to Claire. Then I untied the dogs from the back of the car, locked the car, and wheeled us through the parking lot. Then I ran and walked around the golf course in a three-mile loop.

Claire and Ivy didn't like this whole production at first. They both wondered why we had to do this, with the straps around the body, with no way to get out. For the first half mile, I would have to say, "We *cannot* stop. No one gets out! We have to stay in our seats. Here, do you need more snacks?" But as I started running and the dogs trotted next to me, both on one side, my right hand wrapped with leashes while clutching the stroller bar, the kids would start babbling happily to each other and eating their snacks and watching the world go by.

My dogs didn't like other dogs. Potus had been attacked by three different dogs by then. I didn't let her make eye contact with other dogs if I could help it, because that tended to set the dogs off. Clearly, she was communicating "I am the boss of you" everywhere she went. So sometimes I had to lag behind another jogger with a dog. When other dogs passed us coming the other direction, I had to give the dogs a small tug, warning them to be good. If one of the kids started yelling, we'd have to stop and I'd have to hope that another dog didn't show up suddenly.

There were times when both kids were screaming and the dogs were barking at another dog and also each other, but I'd have to just keep running. If someone had to go potty, that someone had to *hold it the fuck in*. I said as much. There would be no stopping. "No stopping! Can't stop!" I would sometimes yell, seemingly at the air. The four dependents quickly learned that their needs would not be met for the next forty-five minutes. They became more complacent. They stopped asking for stuff.

That was satisfying.

I also enjoyed how the other joggers and walkers at the Rose Bowl could not shut up about the spectacle we created: a gigantic double jogging stroller with a baby and a toddler in it, pushed by a frizzy-haired jogging woman with two large dogs.

"You have your hands full, don't you?" they'd call to me.

"Yep!" I'd yell at them triumphantly. What else was there to say? I was proud of myself.

Normally I didn't do shit. I hated to take the kids to the grocery store alone. I hated to go anywhere. I just wanted to lie around at home and babble at my dependents and eat tasty foods. But I knew I needed to work very hard to prevent myself from becoming sick and unmoored again. I had to dig my fingernails into the ground so I didn't slip off the edge. I had to stop the ground from moving. I would do it. I would survive.

On the last day before Bill returned, I finally lost my cool. I was holding the baby—she was enormous by then, twenty pounds—and Claire was tapping me on the shoulder. Tap tap tap. *Mommy.* Tap tap. The baby felt like three bowling balls in a sack, throwing her weight around and pushing me off balance. Tap, tap. *Mommy. Mommy.*

"HEY. Claire. Do you see what I'm dealing with here? I have my hands full, okay? Can you see with your eyes what is going on? Make an adjustment!" I talked to Claire like she was my thirty-five-year-old coworker. She wasn't even three yet.

I remember that moment so clearly. I remember how annoyed I was with Claire. I remember thinking she was being absurdly irrational and impossibly unfair to me. All of the victorious jogging in the world can't erase that.

I wasn't at my best that year. When you're struggling just to get through the day, you lose sight of the big picture. But when I look at old photos of me and Bill and the babies from that year, I'm confused. We look relaxed and happy. The house always looks spotless. I always think I ignored my kids too much, because they were in day care and I had a full-time job and so did Bill. I can't remember sitting around the house staring at them. But our videos tell a different story. Everyone is talking at once, and I'm often the one listening, asking questions, goofing around with them. Or I'm watching someone dance. Or I'm dancing. Or we're all dancing.

Life was a party all along. The kids were happy and the state of our marriage was strong. The walls weren't falling sideways. No bombs were exploding. It only felt like the world was ending. It was all in our heads.

PART III

11

The Suburbs

What are the suburbs? I thought they were small, leafy towns within reach of the city. I was wrong. Bill and I had been living in a small, leafy town just north of Los Angeles. Our town was filled with urban types of people, hipsters and weirdos, creative people and sloppy freaks and other human beings who have "I reject the dominant paradigm" written all over their faces.

The suburbs aren't filled with people like that. At first, it can be hard to tell the difference. You think you're moving from one small town on the outskirts of the city to another. But soon you realize that you've moved a few miles too far. You're in the suburbs now. Nothing is the same.

The suburbs are a place where people go to embrace the dominant paradigm, because the dominant paradigm makes them feel safe and comfortable. People who've grown tired of the big city move there because they're sick of noise and graffiti and cigarette butts in the gutter. Or they move there because the parking is easier and there's a really big Target and a Panera and a HomeGoods, all right next to each other.

Lots of people hate the suburbs for many good reasons. Bill and I might've understood that, had we paid attention to the fifty-odd years of negative literature on the subject. Instead, we preferred to invent reality inside our heads. So we became the first humans ever to move to the suburbs without knowing what the suburbs actually were.

The irony of living among people who place peace and quiet at the top of their priority list is that they're often very angry. Now, I'm sure that makes you think of all the angry people on your Nextdoor site in your small town or your urban neighborhood. Trust me, you don't know anger until you witness suburban anger up close.

In the suburbs, people are angry at the guy from the gas company who walks up and brazenly checks their gas meter. The audacity of this man! They're angry at the water company, which is staffed by ineffectual scammers, and they're enraged at the water board, which raised rates for the fourteenth year in a row because they're greedy, bad people. They're angry at the woman from the cable company because she's actually a criminal, scoping out their houses, trying to find a way inside, so she can steal their old Tupperware and their brown corduroy armchairs and the shelving for their entertainment systems—all of which she could get for free on Nextdoor any day of the week, since everyone's always trying to foist their ugly furniture onto someone else. But then they get angry when the people who said they'd take their furniture never show up to get it. Then they're angry when the junk pickup truck never arrives. But they're also livid when their neighbors put their stuff out on the curb, because that's trashy and it drives down the property values in the area. But they're *also* angry that property values are going *up* in the area, because who can afford to live here anymore?

And once these suburb dwellers discover that the woman from the cable company wasn't a criminal, she was actually from the cable company, are they less angry? No. They're still enraged, about coyotes and littering and teenagers and off-leash dogs. They're infuriated by traffic and closed stores and new stores and too many stores and not enough stores. They're pissed off about danger and people who drive too fast and also traffic that slows you down too much. They're miffed by power shortages and cable outages and junk mail and solicitors and 5G and anti-vaxxers and tree huggers and fascists and brown-skinned people whose behavior "seems suspicious." They're mad about people who make everything about politics and people who are ignorant about politics and people who feed the coyotes and clog up the streets with traffic and drive too fast and don't vote and do vote, but for the wrong person.

In my particular suburb, every other lawn seems to have a little sign with a cartoon of a dog taking a shit on it, under the words PLEASE CLEAN UP AFTER YOUR DOG. But oddly enough, there's also dog shit all over the place. So everywhere you go, all you see is dog shit flanked by little cartoons of dogs shitting. After a while, it can be hard to know who to hate more, the people letting their dogs shit all over the place or the people thrusting their shitting-dog cartoons in your face at every turn. Before you know it, you're angry at *everyone*. You don't even know why.

One afternoon I was walking my dogs and a man in a pickup truck pulled up next to me, rolled his window down, and yelled, "Pick up your goddamn dog shit!"

"You mean back there? She was just peeing!" I told him. At the time, Potus's bad back meant that she looked a lot like a shitting-dog cartoon whenever she peed. So I pulled some poop bags out of my fanny pack and waved them around as proof. "See? Believe me, I always clean up after my dog!"

The guy just sat there looking at me, trying to process the incomprehensible fact that he had nothing to be angry about. "All right, then," he mumbled. But by then, *I* was starting to feel a little angry, not just because I'd been misunderstood and yelled at, but also because I had become the kind of woman who wears a fucking fanny pack full of poop bags and explains her dog's peeing habits to a stranger. But life in the suburbs has a way of demeaning you no matter what you're doing. The suburbs are supposed to fix everything, but instead, the suburbs make everything worse. You never escape with your dignity intact.

Expecting a place to fix everything is obviously a recipe for disaster. But maybe you hated people to begin with, hence your movement away from a dense urban hub. You wanted some control over your environment. You didn't want to circle for blocks looking for a parking space or worry about crime. And as much as you hate coyotes and rats and other creatures, maybe you hated other people the most. You were trying to get away from hipsters, vaping and throwing parties and acting a little too carefree, mostly because they made you feel so old. But now you're surrounded by *actual* old people, yelling about crimes that you and the gas company guy didn't commit.

In other words, the suburbs are designed to make you hate yourself.

∞

I loved the little house in Highland Park I owned when I met Bill. Sadly, the local elementary school down the street from my house was widely agreed to be terrible—not just a little bit bad, but abysmal. So we enrolled Claire in a very cool, very hip progressive private school in a nearby upscale town. We couldn't really afford the tuition, but we couldn't resist the smart, engaged progressive teachers who taught there. Plus they had a vibrant arts program and a wonderful music program where they sang classic songs like "This Land Is Your Land" with gusto. It was a tasteful, robust place, this school. They spoke in gentle tones there, but said wise things. Everyone loved reading books, everyone loved kids, everyone was eco-aware and exceptional and charming and *just right*.

Then we went to an open house and it was awful. It wasn't the teachers, they were great. It wasn't the kids, they were precocious and delightful. It was the parents. The parents were unbearable. They were all attractive and well-dressed. They all spoke in polite tones and seemed professional. They all made healthy incomes at their respectable, thriving careers. I could almost picture their houses full of mid-century modern furniture. I could almost hear the hum of their Nespresso machines. I could almost see them talking to their friends about how much they loved *The Wire*. I could picture Jonathan Franzen and Zadie Smith on their bookshelves, and taste the home-brewed beer they served at their barbecues—*Dave's been getting into home brewing, did I mention that? Yeah, it's pretty cool.* It was all pretty cool, very cool. It was "a cool little school"—that's how one friend put it, a friend I sort of liked and also sort of hated. A cool little school. She was the kind of person who was extremely anxious about doing anything that wasn't cool. I really hated her a lot, now that I think about it. I just didn't realize it back then.

We left the open house and got into the car, and the first thing Bill said was "Jesus Christ. Those *people.*" He said this in the tone of Marlon Brando hoarsely whispering "The horror!" in *Apocalypse Now.*

I knew exactly what he meant. Those precious, precious people. There was just no way we could tolerate seeing their well-groomed, tasteful faces every day. There was no way we could hear them murmuring to their adorable children about making good and bad choices. We could not listen to a mother telling her kindergartner with the pink mohawk and the London Calling T-shirt, "Check your body" and "See how your body is feeling." Bill and I longed to hear words like "Stop it" and "Do you need a time-out right now?" and "Go somewhere else for a minute."

It wouldn't be fair to our kids, to raise them around grade-school-age kids in Led Zeppelin T-shirts and tiny little Doc Martens. Our kids deserved better than that. Our kids deserved the comfort of mediocrity.

$$\infty$$

Around this time, we found ourselves taking a walk through a park after dinner at our favorite Mexican restaurant, north of Glendale. The sun was setting on the mountains in the distance. A Little

League baseball game was underway. We stopped to watch for a minute. We might've recently consumed one or possibly two very strong margaritas. There was pop music playing, cheerful and unpretentious. Burly basic-bitch dads in cargo shorts were encouraging their kids to focus and hit the damn ball very hard without asking them to search inside themselves for some answer regarding whether or not they were fully committed to the sport of baseball. Moms with bright orange hair and a solid inch of gray roots were texting their friends on their extra-large rhinestone-encrusted phones instead of watching the game.

What was *this magical place?* we wondered. *Had we stumbled on paradise?*

At that moment, having just poured an indeterminate volume of tequila down our gullets, we could've wandered into a satanic ritual and immediately pledged our souls and the souls of our children to the devil. Instead, we decided to move to the suburbs. Same thing, pretty much.

$$\infty$$

When I first toured our house in the suburbs, I once again thought I had stumbled on paradise. It was a clear fall day. The grass looked so green outside, the mountains in the distance so idyllic. The house was right across the street from a high school, but when I walked in and saw the view out of the big picture window, I was seduced. It was a beautiful high school: two stories, high ceilings, and a big traditional front lawn. My own high school was just a cluster of squat brick buildings looking out on a giant parking lot, but this one was like the dream high school from *Grease*. You could imagine kids singing songs about being friends forever on the grass out front. And maybe people *did* stay friends forever, out here in the suburbs. Maybe living here would feel more authentic and wholesome, like stepping back in time. Life would finally feel *real*!

But the pool in the house's backyard was the biggest surprise of all. It had rock walls and was surrounded by bamboo that needed to be watered constantly in order to stay green. There was a waterfall that led to a moat that ran directly outside the back door. You had to cross into the backyard by walking on a little bridge over a pond. It was all so breathtakingly impractical: a verdant miniature Hawaiian rain forest, on the outskirts of arid LA, with two feet of water right outside the back door for the baby to fall into and drown.

I couldn't resist. A sensible mom would never purchase this foolish property, with its backyard of death traps. And there was nothing I wanted to avoid more than becoming a sensible mom. You could never create this kind of wasteful backyard wonderland in a hip urban neighborhood, flanked by neighbors with yards full of native plants on drip systems. This house was an aberration. This house gave the desert the finger. This house said "Fuck you, arid coastal ranges, I built a *lagoon*."

I pictured myself lounging next to my own private grotto with a fruity, umbrella-festooned cocktail in my hand. (This is the lasting legacy of the 1980s Ricardo Montalbán–led escapist drama *Fantasy Island*: to a whole generation of middle-class humans, living the good life is as simple as putting a tiny umbrella in your drink.) I pictured my friends receiving their fruity cocktails like guests on *Fantasy Island*. "Smiles, everyone! Smiles!" I pictured them gasping at the tacky horrors of my boldly distasteful suburban home.

This is what I wanted: to leave the reach of the city, but to remain *within reach* of the people who lived there. I wanted to show my urban friends a superior way of life. It wasn't all about mid-century modern furniture! The good life was super cheesy, actually! And I'd educate my fellow suburb dwellers on food and culture that's superior to anything they might be getting at the Habit or Panera or, you know, the cafeteria at Ikea.

In other words, I was exactly as deluded as the crow that lived in the backyard. It sat on the roof deck. It perched on the chairs in the backyard. But the main draw was the pool: it drank and also cleaned whatever it ate in the overflow between the hot tub and the pool. It figured flowing water must be clean, healthy water. It looked good, so therefore it must *be* good.

It wasn't until the last days of escrow that we discovered that the owners of our new house had a live-in maid named Maria who watered everything by hand, every day. This explained the lack of sprinklers on a timer around the pool, and the total lack of sprinklers in the front lawn. During our final walkthrough, the owner told us, "People ask us why we never got a dishwasher, and we always say, 'We don't need one. We have Maria!'"

They kept the pool heated to 90 degrees most of the time, he told me. (I later discovered that heating the pool to that temperature adds $100 to your gas bill each time you do it.) They had a tropical fish tank built into the wall that offered a view from the den into what would become our bedroom. "We have a fish guy who cleans the tank once a month and he only charges a hundred," the owner said, as if hundred-dollar bills were falling from the sky. They offered to pay for the fish guy for the first year, so they didn't have to remove the fish tank.

I was game. The tank was yet another wildly impractical fea-ture I loved about this tacky paradise, yet another hedge against the pragmatism of marriage and kids. But Bill said no way, *no way* were we keeping the tank and the fish and the fish guy. Bill was allergic to having a fish guy. He was also allergic to dying fish and invasive species of plants and men with live-in maids. But I was optimistic that I could figure out how to keep the fish alive once the fish guy's free year ran out. How hard could it be? It would be worth it, to bring people to the house and show them the fish in the wall.

I also wanted to get an obscenely large flat-screen TV. I wanted to install a swim-up bar out back. I wanted speakers blasting Dr. Dre around the clock. Somehow the suburbs would keep me from becoming a boring mom. I would become something else instead, something a little wilder and trashier. Who cared what? As long as it wasn't dull and predictable.

I wanted to live among these deeply unhip middle-class families—Korean and Mexican and Armenian and white. They were everywhere, taking their kids to Little League, strapping their kids into high chairs at the local restaurants, pushing their strollers down the street at the farmer's market. They wore baseball hats and Dockers and heavy mascara and tube tops. They talked about Disneyland unironically. There were trees everywhere, and there was no graffiti. It looked good, so it must *be* good.

This is what's known as irrational exuberance. It leads you to overvalue things that are probably not quite as amazing as you think. But at the time it made perfect sense. We would sell our tiny house, packed with loud babies and animals, and move into a bigger house with a view of the mountains. We would enroll our kids in public school, where they would be mildly neglected in the same ways that we ourselves had been mildly neglected as children. In suburban public schools, our offspring would never hear about choices, they'd only hear words like "STOP MOVING!" and "BE QUIET!" and "YOU CAN'T EAT THAT THERE!" In the suburbs, we'd be free to interact with distracted, slovenly savages just like ourselves. We would never have to feel ungroomed or unprofessional or uncool at the school pickup. In the suburbs, we could savor the comfort of our mediocrity together.

Having children unearths your truest desires and fears. Even when you want your children to grow up to be thoughtful, thriving professionals, it seems wrong that they should grow up *among* such people, in the company of wealth and taste and even the faintest hint of competitive spirit. It seems offensive somehow, that they should have friends who know a great deal about homemade sushi or independent filmmakers. Who could stand to have their children mingling with the sorts of kids who've been quietly learning Italian on their iPhones? Bill and I had reverse status anxiety. We didn't want to compete with anyone. We wanted to pull all of our chips from the game and go home and eat nachos instead.

It seemed better for our kids to grow up around people who were struggling a little just to get along with other people: shy parents and weird parents and sad parents, lots of overworked husbands and lots of exhausted housewives, none of them really connecting with each other that well or talking about their feelings much, or at least that's how it looked to us at the time. It seemed appropriate that, instead of openly addressing their feelings among progressive elites, our kids should grow up barely suppressing their true feelings behind vague but safe language—devoid of meaning, devoid of ideas. "Hey, how's it going? What's new? Jayhawks struggling a little lately. Can you bring a dip to the party? Looking forward to it!"

Our kids should never feel as if they had limitless choices, the way the kids at "cool little schools" surely did. They should be realists, recognizing that their futures were bounded by compromises and hard limits in every direction. They should feel the boundaries of their world pressing in on them. They should learn to make their ideas and feelings and urges very small, shrink them down into a tiny square. "WHAT ARE YOU DOING?" they'll hear. "WHO TOLD YOU YOU COULD DO THAT?" They should have to complete lots of pointless worksheets at school, and be tested repeatedly to see if their spelling really is up to par at age six. They should have teachers who focus primarily on neat handwriting, or who punish their students for every ill-timed bathroom break. Nothing would prepare them for the brutal stupidity of the wider world outside quite like the arbitrary mercilessness of the suburbs.

The suburbs lower your expectations of yourself and others. Suburban parents wear cheap yoga pants to school pickup, and they say things like "Which one is your kid again?" They have outdated shoes and frown lines—like me, like us. They don't put on a smooth professional face in the schoolyard. They look tired. They say things like "Sorry, not much to say this morning." If you throw a dinner potluck because you're tired of cooking for guests, your neighbors will bring a six-pack of beer and a bag of chips, or they'll grab a veggie platter from Costco. If you dare to smash up a few avocados for guacamole at the party, someone will say "Oh my god, why are you going to so much effort?"

No one has extra time or extra money. No one has a hell of

a lot to say. No one is making much of an effort at all. Suburban parents circumnavigate each other, mostly. They avert their eyes, like dogs that are afraid they might rip each other's throats out if they're forced to interact.

Or at least that's how it looks from the outside, before you get to know them. But getting to know them takes a long time—a full decade at least. Until then, the suburbs can make you a little insecure. And then you get angry. And finally, you turn into a complete snob. That's the irony of escaping urban elitism: the consistent mediocrity of the suburbs will make you into *more* of an elitist. You start to look down on the people around you for having the bad taste to live there, *even though they are exactly like you.* So you have to decide that you're better than they are in order to avoid hating yourself. But you still hate yourself. You hated what the Nespresso owners at the private school reflected back at you, but you also hate what the woman buying the two-pound bag of shredded Mexican cheese reflects back at you. You're Holden Caulfield now. You're inferior and superior, like an immature prep school kid, like a self-hating hipster, like a sad suburban newbie on Nextdoor, decrying the dearth of quality pho in the neighborhood.

I once stood in an aisle at the local supermarket while the guy next to me called his wife to report on his shopping progress. "I got the motsa . . . muzza . . . motsyrelly . . . Oh hell, I don't know how you say it, but I got it!" There I was, just sixteen miles north of one of the largest and most culturally diverse cities on the globe, listening to my neighbor mistaking a block of mozzarella cheese for some mysterious import flown in from a far-flung land.

The suburbs could turn anyone into a self-hating elitist asshole, is the point. But Bill and I threw ourselves into suburban life anyway. I knew we would be outsiders if we didn't try very hard to make friends from the start, so we threw birthday parties for the kids and served margaritas for the parents. We threw Fourth of July parties and Superbowl parties. We stood in the concrete schoolyard at the end of the annual fall fundraiser (called *Festi-Fall* or something even worse) and asked, "Who wants to come over to our house for drinks? We're only two blocks away."

And did we love having people over? Did we love cleaning the house and making drinks and running around in circles, trying to seem cheerful and normal-ish? Sometimes. And other times we hated it. Because even though our parenting style was loosely compatible with the parenting styles of the parents we met in the suburbs, we still experienced other people's kids as wild and un-tamed and unrepentant. They spilled their juice boxes all over our house and painted on the bathroom counter upstairs. They got into the pool fully clothed, and instead of getting angry at them, their parents fetched them towels. Their children stared at us with blank eyes when we requested that they stop pounding the piano so loudly or that they relocate to another room.

Bill and I turned into people-pleasing try-hards who scrambled around grilling hot dogs and inflating pool floaties, but we also bellowed at all the kids to simmer down and lamented wet towels on the couch and demanded to know who was fucking with the treadmill again. We were serving up big fake happy chill times, but we had zero chill.

But we *almost* remembered how to have fun, occasionally. Al-most.

Not surprisingly, most of the people we met in the suburbs disliked and distrusted us. Why wouldn't they? We weren't likable or trustworthy. But now I'm getting ahead of myself.

∞

My daughters are going to perform in a piano recital in an old church. After we choose an aisle and sit down, I spot a bee on the floor. I crush it under my shoe. I feel guilty, but you can't have a bee in a church packed with people.

Then I hear a buzzing sound. I look up. There are dozens of bees circling overhead. There are at least fifty bees crawling around on the stained-glass windows nearby. There are bees making their way across the floor, sometimes very slowly, other times skimming erratically toward our feet.

I look around. No one else seems unnerved by the bees. The piano teacher is circulating among the crowd to warn the performers that C2 is silent, so they'll have to use C1 instead. She says nothing about bees. The other families around us sometimes turn their heads to look at the bees, but say nothing.

I look down at my program. The list of performers is very long, suggesting an hour and a half of sitting in the middle of a bee swarm, listening to beginning piano students plink away.

We move to the front of the church. Through the first few performances, a high buzzing sound is all I can hear. A bee bounces off Bill's shirt. During the fourth performance, a bee is crawling slowly across the floor about two feet away. It makes a fast, straight beeline for us (hence the name). I use my program to push it gently in the opposite direction. Ivy whimpers. "I don't like when they slide like that," she says. "It's weird."

"They're all acting strange," I say. "Maybe they're dying." I am trying to sound calm and cheerful about the fact that we're surrounded by desperate, doomed creatures.

It's Claire's turn to play. I start recording her performance on my iPhone, then I feel something on my foot. A bee is sitting on my shoe. I shake my foot. The bee holds on. I shake it again. The bee flies away. The footage of the performance includes a full minute of tile floor.

By the end of the recital, I'm exhausted. But the worst part isn't the bees. The worst part is that no one ever stands up and says "Sorry about all the bees!" No one acknowledges the difficulty of remaining silent in a dark building that's packed with stinging insects.

Later we stand next to a card table outside, eating dry, crumbly chocolate chip cookies someone made. That's life in the suburbs: pretending that nothing is bothering you while you eat something shitty. No wonder I'm constantly disappointed. We moved here to get away from the stress of the city and be a part of a real community. Being part of a community turns out to include countless hours of trying to look relaxed while you freak out on the inside. If you don't stay quiet, if you dare to scream or fidget or complain, you risk everything. Moving to the suburbs means agreeing not to mention that the sky is falling.

But once it became clear that the bees weren't stinging anyone, shouldn't I have stopped panicking? Wouldn't a normal person have acclimated to her circumstances more quickly?

And shouldn't I have adapted to this godforsaken place by now? If I had known the suburbs would be this uninspired, I might not have moved here. If I knew about the bees beforehand,

I might've stayed home. But I would've felt conflicted: There are bees, but we still have to go? That's crazy! Who would expect us to tolerate such a thing? Yet I would also doubt myself: I'm going to miss my kids' recital over this?

These sorts of dilemmas bubble up constantly in the suburbs: Can we really make our daughters skip something called the Daddy-Daughter Dance when they're excited to go? Do we have to watch our kid play soccer when she's just starting to figure out that she hates it? Am I a bad parent if I don't go to the end-of-the-soccer-season pizza party because Round Table Pizza makes me claustrophobic and I don't like the coach that much?

It's true that I'm a little bit more allergic to bees than most people. But the suburbs have taught me that I'm allergic to lots of stuff. I don't like traffic or stale bread or kids who jump on the couch and their parents never tell them to stop. I don't like feeling underslept or going too long without a meal or listening to a gaggle of forty-year-old moms talking about taking pole-dancing classes for exercise ("There should be a way that our husbands can watch us!"). I don't like amusement parks or indoor malls or huge groups of erratic kids or school principals who sound like Lisa Simpson. I reflexively dislike anyone who says things like "Enjoy your summer!" in a loud broadcast-journalist voice. I don't like painting plaster piggy banks or shoving stuffing into an ugly teddy bear at the mall and calling it a craft. I am afraid of tornadoes and people who talk about their kid's Kumon classes. I worry about stampedes and structural failures and terrorists and high school boys with stickers on their cars that say "No Fat Chicks" on them. I hate bad frozen yogurt and the word *froyo*. I don't like long lines or crowds or VOL-LEYBALL MOM magnets on minivans.

I don't even like piano recitals, if I'm being honest. Am I the problem here? Do I hate everything?

$$\infty$$

A few nights before Trump was elected, I went out for drinks with some of the moms I knew, and one of the moms got to talking about the Muslims who were going to flood over the border by the millions if Hillary Clinton became president. I asked her, "Which border?" She seemed to think that Muslims were sneaking in from Mexico. I told her that was not accurate. I told her that Muslims weren't a threat to anyone. I was not that polite about it. I told her that Donald Trump was both a racist and a complete fucking idiot. Some of the moms who were listening nodded along but said nothing. Others said, "No, they're *both* bad. Trump and Hillary are *both* disgusting. *Hillary Clinton makes me sick.*"

When I got home that night, I told Bill I was worried about the election. I thought Trump could win after all. Four days later, Trump won.

In spite of my best intentions to bite my tongue instead of taking my anger out on the people around me, I got a little hostile on Facebook. A few of my kids' friends' moms stopped talking to me. When I showed up at the schoolyard, they averted their eyes and pretended I wasn't there.

I felt like a crow who'd been drinking chlorinated water for years without even knowing it. Suddenly it felt like *everything* was wrong. Everything in the suburbs seemed pathetic and fake and compromised. Our pool struck me as obscene. The fact that my kids knew all the Disney Channel shows and had seen both Lego movies and had great volumes of Katy Perry lyrics memorized now looked like a living testament to our laziness and bad taste as parents. I'd wanted my kids to understand mainstream American life, to enjoy it. But now that felt like a big mistake.

Why were we living this way without questioning it? I had always prided myself on not being a snob, refusing to draw arbitrary lines between high and low culture. But did we really belong in this place, where people passively nodded along with each other because they often knew, behind their pinched smiles, that they disagreed?

I wanted to move back to the city. Claire burst into tears when she overheard me talking to Bill about it. She and her friends were going to go to junior high and high school together, she said. They were going to be friends *forever*.

That's what I'd wanted for her. It was my idea. I had filled my church with bees, and now I had to sit in it—calmly and quietly, never letting on for a second that I wanted to run away, screaming.

For the first time in my life, I couldn't run away. I was stuck.

$$\infty$$

Being stuck forces you to learn. Bill and I had no choice. We had to adjust to our surroundings. We had to drink chlorine and pretend it wasn't poisoning us.

And slowly, we could recognize that not everyone was terrible. There were good things about the suburbs. People could seem fake, but they didn't really bullshit you. And they didn't make things more complicated than they actually were. They mostly wanted you to keep things simple, too.

People who live in my particular middle-class suburb don't crave status, for the most part. They don't judge you based on how you dress or how your house looks. They don't pretend they're better than they are. They don't imbue fashion and design choices with great weight and meaning. They're not remotely anxious about seeming cool. They talk openly about sex and express a lot of gratitude for their spouses. When they're going through something difficult, they usually say so up front.

In other words, people in the suburbs aren't so guarded after all. You just have to pretend that you're totally uninterested, and then they'll tell you everything.

And in spite of what you read on Nextdoor, people in the suburbs have a lot of self-control and don't overthink things as much as we do. They can sit in the middle of a bee swarm without reviewing all of the bad choices that led them to that fateful place. I was the one who was deeply conflicted. I kept telling myself that I wanted our lives to be ordinary, but some part of me didn't want to be ordinary at all.

Where does anyone belong? And why did it matter so much to me, to feel like I fit in? I'm not sure. All I know is that it's hard to make choices that make sense for you and your husband *and* your kids. It's hard not to feel like you're messing it all up. Everything feels personal, and everything leaves a mark.

$$\infty$$

After they took the fish tank out of the wall and moved out, the couple who sold us their house moved to a smaller house in Arizona and took Maria with them. Two years later, the man died in a car accident. A teenager was speeding recklessly and swerved over the median and his car hit the man's car, killing him and his brother before they could even be flown to the local hospital.

Our house represents the happiest years of his life. He probably didn't think it would end up that way. He probably thought this was just somewhere he'd lived for a while. He was going to end up somewhere much better. But this was the summit for him. This house in the suburbs was as good as it got for him.

And one day, this house in the suburbs might just represent the happiest years of our lives, too. You never want to believe that you don't have control over these things. You want to feel like the future is limitless, and you can write your own ending.

Is this really as good as it gets? I sometimes found myself wondering. *Because I'm pretty sure I want more than this.*

12

Highway to Hell

Surrendering to the suburbs felt natural at first, like falling into a big squishy couch. In fact, the first thing I bought when we moved in was a giant overstuffed sectional that filled up the whole den, plus a flat-screen TV and an expensive sound system to go with it. When I got home from the audio store, I told Bill I'd spent our entire home improvement budget. We didn't have any money left for other fixes, so we'd have to live with the weird black toilet in the downstairs bathroom, the old vinyl flooring in the bedroom, the stained white wall-to-wall carpeting upstairs, the hideous white vinyl garage door . . . the list went on and on. We would paint the walls and tolerate the ugliness until we had enough saved to do more.

Bill wasn't angry that I'd blown everything on a couch and a TV. Those purchases reflected our shared values at the time: I was a full-time TV critic, and we'd spent the first years of our relationship in bed, watching TV. Overspending on the TV wasn't only a way of honoring our core principles as a couple, it was a rare moment of impulsive indulgence that just felt *right*. We'd both spent a lifetime being too hard on ourselves. Making sloppy, irrational choices sometimes felt like our shared way of letting ourselves off the hook and doing something odd that only the two of us could possibly see as a reasonable choice.

But if I'm being fair, Bill has always encouraged my more impulsive choices, whereas *his* more irrational decisions tend to send me into a tailspin. And as the kids got bigger and learned to use words, whimsical choices—and the messiness and fallout from those choices—weren't just a challenge for two people to work through. Suddenly we had to negotiate with a whole room full of volatile beings— *intelligent* volatile beings who couldn't necessarily solve the problem at hand, but *definitely* knew whose fault it was we were in such a mess.

When chaos ensued, instead of just apologizing to one person, Bill and I found ourselves apologizing to three humans—and sometimes two dogs as well. The crushing guilt of screwing things up became a significant factor in both of our lives. Neither of us did well with guilt as it was. Guilt kicked up our tendency to blame someone else for whatever shitstorm we happened to be in at the moment. And blame took the shitstorm from a Cat 1 to a Cat 5 in seconds.

When you live at the center of a volatile community in emotional hurricane country, you take fewer risks. You choose safe activities, become creatures of habit, hunker down, and minimize negative stimuli. You work against your impulses and stick to what's already worked—to prevent a meltdown, to avoid crises, to stay on each other's team.

That's *mostly* how we lived, anyway.

∞

We are stuck in bumper-to-bumper traffic in the middle of no-where, sixteen hours from home.

I am trying very hard not to blame Bill for this, despite the errors in his judgment that got us here. It's not his fault that we're packed into a minivan, crawling along in two-mile-per-hour traffic on some godforsaken stretch of highway in the middle of Texas with our four female dependents, ages eight, seven, six, and three. It's certainly not his fault that the two oldest, most mature dependents lack opposable thumbs, are not tax-deductible, and are shed-ding all over the back of the vehicle. It's also not his fault that the two younger dependents require restroom stops so frequent that it's steadily eroding my will to live.

It isn't Bill's fault that two of the dependents in the minivan do not understand language, or that a third dependent vacillates between verbal and preverbal communication, depending on her state of mind. Nor is it his fault that all four of the four dependents are whining, each at a different pitch, intensity, and volume.

But for some reason, it *does* feel like Bill's fault that the loudest of the four dependents needs to go to the bathroom. She needs to go to the bathroom *right now*.

I check the GPS on my phone and see a long stretch of red in-terstate, an inexplicable logjam in the middle of nowhere.

"It goes on for four miles. I don't get it. There's nothing here."

Bill looks at the kids in his rearview mirror. "Listen, you guys? We're going to be moving this slowly for a while—we won't even reach the nearest exit for like an hour. So you need to just focus on something else so you can hold it in until we get there."

"Nooo, I can't! I need to *poop* right now!"

The word *poop* instantly moves the chorus of whines up a

register, like the dramatic key change at the end of a Disney ballad. But there is no way we're pulling over right now. There's not a tree or bush to hide behind for miles. Wrenching this particular dependent out of the car, into the cold winter air, and asking her to pull her pants down and squat in a ditch in full view of twenty cars? It isn't an option.

This is the moment we've been training for, I think. This is the moment that tests our mettle as parents, as people, as fearless leaders.

I shift into crisis mode. Crisis mode is cheerful and calm. Crisis mode, in this case, includes an upbeat, lighthearted narrative about how it's no big deal to squat in the back of a moving minivan in the middle of Texas in order to defecate into a doggie waste bag. Doing so is not only private (relative to mooning two dozen interstate travelers), but it's also safe (we are inching along at walking speed) and sanitary (compared to your average gas station bathroom, which we can't get to regardless). It also obviates the need for either crapping in your pants or wiping your butt on some loose gravel and then sprinting to catch up with the minivan.

My speech is rousing, so rousing that someone who didn't know any better, someone from a foreign country or distant planet, might come away thinking that people shit into each other's hands in moving vehicles all the time, just for fun.

But the dependent in question shakes her head. She is *not* taking a dump in the back seat of the minivan. She is not *an animal*, like some of these other passengers. She needs a bathroom, not a poop bag.

Ten minutes later, through tears, she agrees to try. A doggie bag is held open, very wide. No! She can't do it. It's too terrible. She returns to her seat and is strapped in again.

Five minutes after that, she yells out in agony. A catcher's mitt is fashioned out of paper towels. A second attempt is made. But let's be honest. Despite the courageous, happy tone, many images are floating through our fearless leader's mind as she holds the mitt in position. They are catastrophic images. The other dependents must be imagining some of the same things, because all three of them have become quiet and are averting their eyes, turning their gazes toward the barren landscape. One of the three announces that this wretched place is the hometown of former president George W. Bush Jr.

There is a moment of total silence. You could hear a pin drop. You could hear something a little heavier than a pin drop. Next, a flurry of wrapping and double bagging and triple bagging ensues. Toilet paper and antibacterial gel and antiseptic wipes are dispatched. Then, more antibacterial gel, until everything and everyone in the van is coated in a thin layer of disinfectant. The windows are rolled down, and a refreshing wave of winter air wafts through, sending a few stray dog hairs floating out across the Texas plains.

Once the windows are rolled up again, the passengers, perhaps invigorated by the cold air, marvel at the lack of a lingering stench, the lack of mess, the lack of any other ill effect. The dependent in question announces that she feels way, *way* better. A strange sense of calm and borderline elation sets in.

"That made the whole trip totally worth it," Bill says as I climb back into the passenger seat. That's how your mind works when you've been driving for sixteen hours. Shitting in the car equals making memories that last a lifetime.

I feel proud of myself for being so calm and persuasive. But even as I'm congratulating myself for pulling it off without a hitch, some sick part of my brain says to me, "This whole thing is *all his fault.*"

∞

Two days before, we were booked on a plane to the Raleigh-Durham airport in North Carolina, departing from Los Angeles International Airport at six in the morning. At 4:00 a.m., Bill was charged with walking the dogs, briefly, to encourage them to do their business, since they'd be locked in the house until my brother picked them up early that afternoon. Unfortunately, Bill didn't drink any coffee before he left with the dogs. He lost track of time. He also may have lost track of his name and address and what the fuck he was supposed to be doing out there in the dark. After thirty minutes of wondering what was taking him so long and loading up the car with suitcases and sleeping kids all by myself, I finally remembered that he might have his cell phone on him. I took a deep breath. I would handle this diplomatically, so as not to upset the children.

"Where the *fuck* are you?"

"The stupid dogs won't take a shit!"

"WE NEED TO LEAVE RIGHT NOW," I bellowed into the phone.

Bill returned five minutes later. We locked the house. I spent the first ten minutes of our drive to the airport hissing at him that if he's fucking senile without his fucking coffee, then *obviously* he should drink his fucking coffee before he wanders around in the dark with the dogs and makes us miss our fucking flight. He spent that time hissing back that I should stop freaking out over nothing, and there was no fucking way we would miss our flight.

Then we drove in silence. I tried to breathe deeply. I pictured us making our flight, no problem.

By the time we made it to the packed check-in line at the airport, and I saw the sign saying the cutoff for checked bags was forty-five minutes before each departure, I knew we were doomed. As we left the "Check in here" line and moved over to another, less promising line, the kids stopped babbling happily and started to whimper.

"Are we going to miss our flight?" my older daughter asked, her enormous eyes filling with tears.

"You mean we aren't going to Grammy's house for Christmas?" my younger daughter screeched, her face crumpling in despair.

"We might . . . We'll try . . . ," I stuttered. "We don't know yet . . ."

The travelers around me glared. The girls wailed and threw themselves onto the floor, which seemed like an unsanitary choice, but I couldn't intervene. It was pure Greek tragedy. I half expected the travelers around us to form a Greek chorus and explain to all onlookers, in rhyming verse, that they were witnessing a tale of great woe, forged in the lamentable choices of one deeply flawed man, a hapless husband devoid of a frontal lobe.

This was when I shifted from furious-wife mode to fearless-leader-in-crisis mode. "Look, we *will* probably miss our flight. That's how it's looking right now. But listen, that's *okay*! It's totally fine." Crisis mode is resilient and unflappable. "They'll put us on another flight—we'll fly standby."

Yeah. Because when families of four miss their flights out of LAX over the holidays, guess what? It's no problem at all. The major airlines keep four empty seats together on even their most booked planes, just so they can give those seats to the really fucking stupid people who like to stroll their dogs around in the dark for half an hour at four in the fucking morning instead of making it to the fucking airport on time.

I switched gears again. "And if that doesn't work? They'll book us on another flight, maybe one that leaves later tonight or tomorrow. We'll just go home and relax and come back tomorrow."

"I don't want to come back tomorrow! I want to fly to Grammy's house right now!" Both girls were wailing now. We were all sitting on the filthy airport floor, me hugging my crying girls, surrounded by our suitcases in the middle of an unmoving, unhappy line.

"And what if we can't get on another flight?" my older daughter asked, apparently reading my panicked mind. "I want to go to North Carolina *right now*! I don't want to stay here for Christmas."

Under normal circumstances, this is the point when you'd tell your kids to simmer the fuck down and stop acting like lunatics. Were *you* happy about missing your flight? Were *you* happy that you chose to marry a man *without brains inside his empty skull*? No, you were not. But you weren't crying about it. Not yet, anyway.

But these weren't normal circumstances. Heroic words were in order.

"Listen, listen. We are going to North Carolina, no matter what! Okay? If we can't get on a flight, you know what we'll do instead? We'll get in our minivan and just start driving. It's only December nineteenth! That means we have time to get there. And

I've done it before! You just drive east for a long, long time, and eventually, guess what? You get to Grammy's house!"

"I DON'T WANT TO DRIVE! I WANT TO FLY ON A PLANE!"

"I know you like planes. But I just *love* driving across the country, because you get to see the whole entire country, not just a few stupid clouds. You've never even seen the whole country before, have you? It's amazing! The landscape changes constantly. You go through the desert, and then you get to the Great Plains, where Laura Ingalls Wilder lived. You pass through so many different states—New Mexico and Texas and Georgia! It's so relaxing, just looking out the window all day! You wouldn't believe how beautiful the sky looks out there. Especially at six a.m., when you wake up early just to drive? It's all pink and purple and you're listening to good music, and then you stop at McDonald's—they're all over the place, even in the middle of nowhere!—and you eat an Egg McMuffin."

Our fearless leader really likes Egg McMuffins.

And it's true that she also loves driving across the country. I've done it many times before, on nightmarish marathon trips with my family as a kid, with college friends and boyfriends, and once with my oldest dependent, a yellow collie mix who was just eight months old at the time and spent most of the trip with her nose stuck out the window.

This might be why it was so easy to expound on the joys of cross-country travel, to distract the kids as we passed through the snaking security lines, as we watched our first standby possibility go up in smoke, as we stood in a long line for customer service and then went to another gate and failed to fly standby a second time.

At least fifteen other standby passengers were in front of us. We could do this all day long, I thought, and never get on a flight. How would the kids like spending the entire day at the airport, weathering one disappointment after another?

At this point, I took a short break from my narrative so I could step away from the group and cry for a minute or two. I felt so guilty for putting my kids through this trauma and screwing everything up, mostly by marrying a pathetic pea-headed idiot-man. But I couldn't even yell at the pea-headed man, not only because it would upset the kids but also because he obviously knew he was to blame for this mess. He had gone from his original loud this-is-no-big-deal state to a much quieter I-hate-myself-and-want-to-die state, and I needed him to live so that I wouldn't have to take the kids to the bathroom by myself every time.

After a few minutes of sobbing, I pulled myself together and continued my story. It was starting to work, too, because the kids stopped howling and moaning. Instead, the infinite delights of car travel were starting to sink in. The sights! The sounds! The around-the-clock DVDs! The tacky state-shaped souvenirs! The impromptu snacks! "It's a real adventure," I kept saying.

This might be why, by the time all four of us were confirmed on a flight to North Carolina on December 23, both kids were convinced that driving across the country for three days was a much better choice than flying. Who wanted to wait around for four days and *then* fly? That would be torture. Instead, we could go home, grab a few clothes (our bags were on their way to North Carolina already), put the dogs in the car, and go. The dogs wouldn't have to be boarded. We could take them with us! We'd get there even *sooner*. It would be a real adventure.

In other words, sometimes fearless leaders in crisis mode are a little *too* convincing.

∞

The trip was far more harrowing and tedious than I'd made it out to be at the airport. There was a brief period of calm after the unfortunate traffic-jam crisis in Texas, but once we got to Meridian, Mississippi, the mood suffered dramatically. The kids were angry at us for tricking them into such a purgatorial journey.

Bill was in good spirits but had assiduously avoided discussing his early-morning mistake. I knew he was sidestepping the subject because he felt guilty, but I was still annoyed in spite of my best intentions to get over it. After three long days of being gung ho and trying to rally everyone to stay positive and embrace the spirit of adventure, my nerves were starting to fray.

Finally, somewhere in the middle of Alabama, cross words were exchanged. There was some yelling, and some small people learned an important lesson about how yelling is bad, but every now and then *you just can't help it*. Like, for example, when someone does something completely irrational and it has major consequences, but he won't admit it or apologize in a real way? And then he snaps at *you* at the drive-thru? Just for pointing out that maybe a little girl should have oatmeal rather than her third biscuit in three days? For him to be a dick over *that* when you've been *sooooo fucking nice* (pronounced slowly, through gritted teeth) for days now? That's called MAKING SOME PRETTY BAD FUCKING CHOICES.

I yelled for a while. At some point, my yelling became almost celebratory. I was enjoying it. I was going beyond the call of duty, yelling-wise.

After that, I cried. The kids were quiet. Finally Bill took a sip of his coffee and then cleared his throat.

"I am sorry about making us miss our flight. I've felt shitty about it this whole time."

I took a small nibble of sausage biscuit.

"I actually have felt incredibly grateful that you shifted into high gear at the airport," Bill said, "because I could barely function. I was paralyzed by self-loathing."

"Yeah, that's why I stepped up. I could tell you felt terrible and could barely deal."

Bill reached for my hand.

I apologized to the kids for getting so angry. Then I mimicked myself yelling. Bill and I laughed at some of the dumb stuff I said. I had pushed it beyond all logic and into the realm of pure blame.

"See, you guys? This is why it's so important to talk about your feelings as they come up, instead of sitting on them," I yelled into the back seat. "Because if you hold them in for too long, they explode all over the place at the worst possible time!"

I turned around to see how this was landing. Both girls had their headphones back on, watching *The Little Mermaid* again.

Everything felt lighter and happier after that. Okay, Potus didn't feel much better. In fact, she looked pretty upset for several miles and refused to chew on the rawhide she was offered, leaving her far less sensitive canine peer to steal it for herself.

But by the time we arrived at my mom's house in North Carolina and were assigned to an upstairs bedroom—with the kids on an air mattress and the dogs in their beds on the floor, every inch of space covered by some living being, every night a chorus of snores—we were used to it. We slept soundly. It almost seemed crazy, letting your four dependents sleep in separate rooms, away from you. We had become a peaceable tribe.

After Christmas, we still had to drive another three thousand miles to get home.

The trip back was not without incident. The windshield wipers malfunctioned in the middle of a rainstorm in Birmingham. In a particularly disgusting gas-station restroom just past Shreveport, the seat fell off the toilet. In a restaurant parking lot outside Dallas, my younger daughter refused to put her shoes on, so she had to spend some tense time in the car with me and the dogs, while my husband and older daughter ate some unexpectedly good Mexican food inside.

Even so, we got better at our traveling routine. The kids mostly slept through the night. The dogs stopped growling at every sound from the neighboring motel rooms. We learned to scout ahead for local restaurants on our phones. We made the kids look out the window for a few hours in the morning, and we figured out a way to get them to nap every afternoon—by telling a story, but only when everyone's eyes were closed.

The kids saw the Mississippi River for the first time and were excited to see it again on the way back. They ate their first fried-chicken biscuit in Louisiana. We played I Spy and sang along to Katy Perry songs. We each had a giant steak at a good steakhouse in Abilene on New Year's Eve, and on the first morning of 2013, we ate waffles shaped like the state of Texas. By the time we reached the border of California, we were starting to see the trip not as a catastrophe but as a smashing success.

To be fair, we also ate a ton of junk food. My older daughter watched the first *Harry Potter* movie nine times in a row. My younger daughter subsisted primarily on chicken nuggets. I gained ten pounds from sitting still for two weeks, only exerting myself to stuff more fried chicken and biscuits into my face. If we'd continued traveling for just a few more days, we all might've become anemic.

Instead, we pulled up to our house in Los Angeles on January 2, just as the sun was setting, exhausted and relieved to be home.

But it felt strange to sleep in separate rooms. It seemed odd to wake up the next morning without hitting the road. I missed being packed into a small space with everyone. I'd learned a lot about my kids from hearing every word that came out of their mouths for two weeks straight. Usually they're at school and then off in the house somewhere, playing their own games. Thanks to that enforced proximity, we understood each other a little better.

And after the blowout and subsequent apologies in Alabama, I felt grateful for Bill. He took on the whole trip without hesitation, and we operated surprisingly well as fearful leaders and clueless tour guides. We agreed on what was important (locating tasty food, making sure the kids had fun, getting enough sleep), and we agreed on what wasn't (sanitary conditions, privacy, vitamin C).

We also figured out that we didn't necessarily have to play it safe all the time. We could wing it, and even though things would always go wrong, our volatile community would recover soon enough. The world might feel like it was breaking into pieces like a spaceship hitting the atmosphere of a hostile planet, but that was an illusion. We could survive the blast. We just had to hold on tight, take a deep breath, and wait for solid ground to return beneath our feet.

13

Fight Song

The odd pressures of suburban life started to sink in sometime in the spring before the presidential election, and came in the form of a talent show. The year before, my older daughter and her friends in the third grade decided they wanted to perform "It's a Hard Knock Life" from *Annie*. So we met the girls and their mothers at a park one Saturday afternoon, and everyone tried to come up with choreography together. As a former chorus geek, I had a lot of very strong opinions about what the girls should do, but I held back. I had learned to bite my tongue in order to fit in with the mothers around me. By the end of the afternoon, we'd only gotten a few verses into the song, and our time was up. Everyone was worried that there wouldn't be enough time to figure it all out before the talent show auditions a week later.

Bill was out of town, so I went home that night and stayed up late choreographing the performance by myself. I made lists of moves, and made charts of how the girls would transition from one formation to another. The next morning, I taught the routine to my daughter, so she could help me teach it to everyone else a few days later. I emailed everyone and told them this was my plan.

This was out of character for me, as a parent. Not only had I never volunteered to fix the school's shoddy music program, but I also hadn't volunteered for countless pancake breakfasts and movie nights and PTA Festi-Falls. It wasn't just that I felt too busy to do these things. I was also worried that if I did them, everyone would figure out that I wasn't the laid-back, super chill mom I played at birthday parties and school pickup.

I was afraid that if I applied my chorus-geek perfectionism to the talent show, I'd go from Matthew Morrison's supportive chorus teacher on *Glee* to Jane Lynch's tyrannical cheerleading coach, shouting things like "Start over, maggots! Not good enough!" If I cared too much, I would piss off the other parents and the kids would hate me and the whole thing would become an enormous nightmare.

Miraculously, that didn't happen. The girls were energetic and their performance was adorable and perfect, the best act in the whole show by far. Everyone stood and cheered.

So naturally, I had to ruin everything the next year instead.

To be fair, as nine-year-olds, my daughter and her friends chose to sing "Fight Song" by Rachel Platten, the sonic version of a one-thousand-year-long noogie. Where "Hard Knock Life" is aggressive and delightful like a homemade pie in the face, "Fight Song" is all faux inspiration and faux strength, like a 1980s-era Barbie wearing pink boxing gloves and a silk boxing robe with her name in glitter on the back. The first line of the song is "Like a small boat on the ocean, sending deep waves into motion." These are words that even a fourth-grader can't sing with conviction. At one point I asked the kids if they knew what the song was about, and they all shrugged like I had asked them what a boxing-themed Barbie might be fighting for.

But it wasn't just the bad song. Fourth grade marks the birth of self-consciousness. It's awkward and ugly and immediate. Even by the time of the final dress rehearsal, the girls looked half asleep. They were joyless. When I encouraged them to infuse their performance with a little more verve, they stared at me through dull, dead eyes. I had become the enemy. I was not trustworthy. Demonstrating enthusiasm was suspect. Indicating that you had a pulse at all was *very* third grade.

What was I fighting for? At the dress rehearsal, one painfully ill-prepared kid after another took to the stage and summarily underwhelmed everyone present. One girl sang out of beat with her music, and no one corrected her, even after she started over twice. *You are half a beat behind!* a voice in my head bellowed. *Get in the motherfucking pocket!* Another three boys were playing the theme to *Star Wars* all wrong on their horn instruments. How could they mess up a song most of us know better than the sound of our own blood coursing through our hotheaded, perfectionist veins? Like aliens from another planet, they blithely changed the triplet notes to quarter notes. *How is this even happening?* my mind screamed.

When my daughter and her friends got onstage, they didn't sing and dance so much as mumble and gesture dispiritedly. I tried to remain calm. I casually told the kids afterward that they were great, but they needed to throw themselves into it a little more. They pretended not to listen. They couldn't even look me in the eyes, possibly because I was gritting my teeth and my face was a tiny bit red and I was sweating just a little. But still. If they didn't listen to me, who would save them from the horrifying humiliation of non-greatness?!

On the walk home from rehearsal, my daughter said she regretted ever signing up for the talent show in the first place.

I felt sick. This was all my fault. So I gave her contradictory advice. I told her everything would be fine, she just needed to care *a lot less* about the whole thing. Neither one of us could control what the group did. That was obvious. As long as we lowered our expectations, it wouldn't be disappointing. *Just accept that it will be exactly this bad forever, and then it's all good!* This seemed to have been my strategy ever since we'd moved to the suburbs: every time you feel angry or upset or impatient with what's happening around you, surrender to mediocrity.

My daughter didn't seem to find these words of comfort all that convincing, possibly because I'd been flailing my arms and bellowing like Mike Ditka about the unmatched gravity of the moment just minutes earlier.

So I handled my feelings of disappointment like any mature adult would: by uploading the video of the performance I took on my phone and emailing it to all of the girls' parents as soon as I got home, along with a note written with the urgent tone of a 911 dispatcher. In order to avert disaster, I explained, each and every parent should analyze my footage with their daughters that night, and then have a frank, in-depth discussion about the profound importance of energy and focus and jazz hands.

Because that's what parents love the most. They *love* to get impossibly long, wordy emails from some fucking mom at the school about the deep significance of whether or not their kids flare their fingers to the correct beat. And yes, I recognized even as I was writing the email that I was digging my own grave, a grave that I would never dig out of, no matter how many pancake breakfasts and movie nights and PTA Festi-Falls I donated my (limited) time and (conflicted) energy to. Even as I was writing that email, a little voice inside my head was whispering, *Comin' in hot, Striker!*

But I couldn't pull back on the throttle. I cared too much.

Bill tried to stop me. I told him about the email I'd sent, and his face melted into a concerned parental cringe. I tried to tell him that I made it all okay by saying "Thank you for your help!" and "Best wishes" at the end of my email, but he didn't buy it. He hinted, very gently, that I had made a mistake.

But I couldn't hear him. I was all in. I had turned some invisible corner from ordinary citizen to frantic, frothing zealot. *This wasn't about me, after all!* This was about *quality* and *standards* and *teaching these suburban fuckers a thing or two about greatness!*

This is the trouble with investing in kids—or in anyone or anything, really. You might be (secretly, self-protectively) aiming not to put your entire heart and soul into it. But then one small desire seems to open up to a vast universe of desires. At first, you just want your kid's performance not to suck. You're protecting your daughter from embarrassment, that's all. But then, out of nowhere, you want your kid to understand how it feels to work really hard for weeks at something difficult. You want her to know the satisfaction of getting up on stage and feeling the whole world melt away, and all that's left is the pure exhilaration of the song and its story. You are wide awake and fully alive. You are at the center of everything.

When you slip into that zone, you go from wanting one tiny little thing to wanting everything—for her, for you, for everyone in the auditorium, for everyone on the planet. But mostly it's for your daughter. You want her to feel like this lovable but shabby place, these kind but disappointing mortals, even this faintly hysterical mother and wisely self-censoring father, are not *all* she has. She can transcend this clumsy world filled with hopelessly half-assed people. She can raise her sights higher, and experience something extraordinary.

$$\infty$$

You might think the moral of this story is that I'm too high-strung for the heady world of elementary school talent shows. That's certainly what one of the parents seemed to imply in a text to me after the dress rehearsal. "There isn't anything more for a grown-up to do," she wrote. "The more they take ownership the better." And then she added, "I think it was harder than some of the girls thought it would be."

When I read that note, some voice in my head said, *Yeah, she's right. There really isn't anything more for a grown-up to do.*

But then another voice spoke. It was the ragged voice of a witch who lives in the inky blackness of a hollow tree and is maybe not a grown-up at all. *Yes. Being good is really fucking hard,* said the witch. *But who wants to work less hard and be less good? Not me!* This witch had cultivated a habit of watching *American Idol* from her hollow-tree lair for years. And when she saw the kids who cared way too much sing their heartfelt songs, it made her cry her witchy eyes out. Sometimes it seemed like everyone was trying to fuck it up for those kids: the band's arrangement was awful, the judges' advice was misleading. But somehow the audience always had an innate sense of magic. You could tell when they felt that magic in their bones.

That kind of magic could lift you up above everything else in the world, all of the friends who didn't understand you, all of the parents who didn't listen. The magic let you know that everyone felt the same things, that everyone was fragile and confused and heartbroken underneath their skin.

∞

On the night of the talent show, I wasn't thinking about magic. I was bracing myself, as the curtains parted. I felt like a jerk for leading my poor lambs to the slaughter of public humiliation.

But as the first wobbly-voiced performer fumbled with her microphone, a different sort of magic slowly took over. I could see that these were *charming* flaws I was witnessing—irreplaceable, once-in-a-lifetime sorts of flaws: the triplet-averse *Star Wars* trio, the gymnast who doesn't quite get her handstand vertical, the distorted microphone squeals in the midst of a breathy *Les Misérables* ballad. It was actually the *non-greatness* that made each kid's performance so memorable and unique.

And when my daughter and her friends took to the stage, some of them looking invigorated and thrilled and others looking distracted and self-conscious, I could see that was part of what made them so engrossing. These were the details that could break your heart: The girl who is always off beat. The girl who smiles but never sings. The girl who sings but never smiles. The girl who moves in the opposite direction from everyone else, no matter how many times you correct her. Together, they form a kind of ragged,

vulnerable tribute to being nine years old, awkwardly poised between very young and too old too soon. Together, they represent
how it feels when you're trying to choose between caring too little
and caring too much.

That's how marriage feels, too. At first I just wanted to feel
safe. I wanted to know that there was someone in the world who
would never abandon me. I just wanted security, and company.
And then, when we had kids, I just wanted to keep everyone else
safe and relatively sane. We moved to the suburbs partially to get a
handle on the chaos of kids and dogs. We wanted more space, more
peace and quiet, more of a sense of control over our lives.

But as my kids grew bigger, I was also trying to manage how
much I loved and worried about them. I was reckoning with how
much I depended on Bill—for love, for help, for everything. And
maybe I was trying to avoid overinvesting in another flawed human. Maybe our interdependence felt threatening to me, at some
level.

And I felt overinvested anyway. I cared too much. There was
no way to avoid it. I was trying not to feel fragile in the face of that
investment.

I was in a state that year, when my marriage was strong enough
but still unexpectedly wobbly at times, when our finances were
stable enough but included a growing pile of credit-card debt, when
my friendships with the other suburban parents never felt real or
dependable. Writing long, exasperated emails to strangers was the
tip of the iceberg; I looked unsteady to the people around me because I *was* unsteady. I wasn't used to doubting myself and questioning my own judgment this often, but motherhood and middle
age and living in this hostile-seeming place had eroded my confi-

dence. I was embarrassed that I could discover such unsteadiness in myself at such a late date. I didn't know how to calm down and enjoy my life.

And it felt excruciating to care so much. I didn't want to feel as much as I was feeling that night, crying my eyes out in the elementary school auditorium. I didn't want anyone to know how much I cared.

I would tell you that this was a rare and special moment, and children grow out of this conflicted state soon enough, and so do middle-aged, married women. But the truth is that this uneasy state lasts a lifetime. We try to shake off our most passionate desires, but instead they render us at once anxious and willfully nonchalant, controlling and totally out of control, intent on divesting and overcome by a feeling that this one tiny thing matters more than anything else in the world. It's not that easy to tame your desires. Sometimes you just want more. This is how it feels to be a little kid. This is how it feels to be an adult. Maybe this is just how it feels to be alive. It's hard to back off, to power it down. It's hard not to care way too much.

14

Cheer

I am eating a giant bowl of mashed potatoes covered in melted cheese, and that's normal. It's normal to take five pounds of leftover mashed potatoes from your fridge, grate a pound of cheese on top, microwave it, and then sit on the couch and eat it while staring blankly at the wall. This is how adult human beings eat lunch.

My daughter is trying out for cheerleading this week. They call it "cheer" now, but it's just as bone-chilling as it was when I did it back in junior high school, which they now call "middle school." Back then, I was high-strung and geeky, which they now call "anxious and socially awkward." I wanted to make cheerleading so I could Be Somebody. While I eat six pounds of food for lunch (which they used to call binge eating, but they now call "self-care"), I'm wondering if this is what my daughter wants too.

My daughter didn't sweat much back in elementary school. She effortlessly made lots of ordinary, lovable elementary school friends. But seventh grade is different. You show up to middle

school, and your entire group of friends might be judged as uncool by some other giant group of friends from an ever-so-slightly
more sophisticated segment of your deeply idiotic suburb. You go
to places like Starbucks or the fucking drugstore next to the Starbucks (this is where they hang out now, instead of the Orange Ju-
lius), and even your closest friends are trying to ditch you, and you
are also trying to ditch some of your *other* friends. Everyone is trying to *win*—or "outbeat the rest," as the grammatically challenged
middle-school cheerleaders put it in one of their cheers.

"Junior high is all about ditching and getting ditched," I tell
my daughter and her friend, trying to make the brutal realities of
seventh grade sound faintly sporting instead of torturous. Even
though I called middle school the wrong name again, they nod
vigorously, so I throw in some wisdom about being who you are,
where you are (*I'm an advice columnist, I'm good at this!*). Their eyes
go dead. I wander off in search of a stiff drink instead. Which is
normal.

It's normal to drink when you're forty-eight years old and you're
looking a little grizzled, but you still want to look beautiful—
magically, implausibly beautiful—possibly because you've always
been attracted to the impossible. Some mornings I look in the
mirror and I see Keith Richards. Other mornings I am Burgess
Meredith. I put moisturizer on Burgess Meredith's face anyway,
as if I can transform him into a dewy nymph. I almost savor the
despair of this moment, of wanting something so shallow and out
of reach.

Being in seventh grade isn't so different. You hate it, but you
also love it a tiny bit for the same reasons you hate it—the drama,
the suffering, the competition. But you want to love it *more*. You

want to be the one who is standing in the front, shouting something and looking cute doing it. You want to *outbeat the rest.*

When I was in seventh grade, I had no dance or gymnastics experience, but I wanted the impossible, and so did my best friend. Every day after tryouts, we practiced our cheers and our jumps and yelled at each other "No broken wrists!" and "That looks sloppy, start over!" When we checked the list after school and saw that we made the team, just eight slots available to sixty girls, we screamed and jumped up and down for a long time. We knew that becoming cheerleaders would change everything. We would still be geeks, sure, but we would be *visible* geeks. People would hate us for no reason. That's what we wanted. That is a normal thing to want at that age.

Now that I'm older and I've been hated for all kinds of reasons, I find cheerleading sexist and futile. I also know from personal experience that at least 91 percent of cheerleading coaches are sadists and sociopaths. That's just a wild guess, but it feels statistically bulletproof inside of my head, where I spend most of my time these days. I'm middle-aged, so I have all kinds of baseless and unfair opinions, which people used to call "being fucking delusional" but now refer to as "honoring your truth." When you wake up in the morning looking like Dumbledore, what else do you have, really? You treasure your petty grievances and sweeping generalizations. You hug them close.

But I don't tell my daughter these things. I don't tell her harrowing stories about my high school cheerleading coach, who was a terrifying cross between an enthusiastic real estate agent and Bernadette Peters on a five-day bender. I don't describe how we were forced to practice dangerous stunts in the gym without mats. Girls would be writhing in pain, saying their backs or heads hurt after a fall to the hard gym floor, and our coach would yelp in her scary baby voice, "You're okay, you're fine, get up!"

I also don't tell her how much I loved wearing my uniform to school, or how satisfying it was to get attention from cute boys for the first time ever, after feeling doomed by my giant ugly glasses and unrelenting acne and bad fashion choices for so long. *Outbeating the rest feels pretty goddamn great*, I never say to her. *I strongly recommend it.*

I am being discreet, which is unusual for me. I want to help my daughter make the team. But I also feel like I should've prevented her from landing here, in this stupid predicament in our stupid suburb. Her dance is set to a hip-hop mix that begins with the words "My left stroke just went viral," from "Humble" by Kendrick Lamar, but then it segues into a bad pastiche of watered-down beats that aren't nearly as good as that song. In spite of my misgivings, I am already yelling "No broken wrists!" and "That looks sloppy, start over!"

After a few rounds of this, she's crying. I'm making cheerleading seem impossible. I am the worst kind of mother, a bossy, shallow cartoon. I don't care. I can't stop barking instructions, which seem to be about dancing but really boil down to *how to be visible and cute and win by cheering someone else to victory*. I never in a million years thought I would end up here. "Be humble, bitch, sit down," Kendrick Lamar whispers inside my brain.

My daughter says she'll freak out if she doesn't make the team. This is normal, I think, but my pulse rate goes up anyway. I tell her that she should try on the despair of not making cheerleading right now, and maybe even cry about it, so she's prepared when she sees the list at school and she's not on it. This is terrible advice, advice so shitty that only a professional advice columnist could give it.

"I feel like you don't think I'm going to make it!" she yells at me. She hates me right now. I hate myself, too. All very normal and developmentally appropriate for everyone involved.

It's true that I feel like she might not make cheerleading, for the same reason I feel like I might get crushed by a mile-wide meteor at any second. I've always expected the worst. It's a way of life. I want her to mimic my mindset, the way I mimicked my mother's. That way no one wants something impossible that they can't have. That way no one is ever disappointed. That way everyone aims low, and no one cares too much about something that's out of their control. That way no one cries their eyes out when they read the list after school on Friday. My friend is a counselor at the school and says that it's like the end of the world every year, hallways filled with sobbing girls. They have a nickname for that day. "Dies Dolorem," or something like that. I might've made that up, too.

When you're middle-aged, it's normal to make shit up. It's normal to be cynical about things you used to care about way too much, and it's normal to find yourself seduced by those same things, out of the blue, in spite of your best intentions. It's also normal to aim for the impossible while expecting the worst. I want my daughter to make cheerleading, and I also don't want her to make it. I want her to pick an activity that's much less sexist and futile, but I also want her to outbeat the rest—not *in spite of* the fact that it's absurd and shallow and twisted, but *because of it*.

Contrary to popular wisdom, growing older does not make you less conflicted. In fact, you become more and more conflicted by the second. You can see all sides of any given thing. It's all stupid bullshit and you want all of it, everything, and you also want none of it, it can all go fuck itself. You are Walter fucking Matthau, and that's delightful in its way, but you also want to be Meryl Streep or Chrissy Teigen or Beyoncé instead.

And let's be honest. As I grew older, I started to feel more competitive, instead of less. I started to want to take more for myself, to indulge myself for a change. Maybe I saw it as a market correction to a lifetime of getting less than I needed: less attention, less approval, less reassurance, less comfort. Adaptive animals learn to comfort themselves.

Sometimes that means discovering that you're ravenous for more. Sometimes that means resolving to take whatever you want for a change. Every pig in shit has its own array of rationalizations: *Maybe I deserve more than most. Maybe I shine more when I take more. Who would I be without too much? Maybe I just want more. Isn't that okay? Why should I always be the one who's generous, the one who's fine with less?*

Maybe this is just where most mothers land, after almost a decade of treating self-sacrifice as their first priority in life. I was becoming more selfish and more conflicted the older I got.

When you're conflicted, it sets people's nerves on edge, particularly when those people are eleven years old and they've been practicing toe-touch jumps for three hours straight. That's when you have to watch your step, or you might start spouting some of your baseless and unfair opinions or airing your petty grievances, the ones you love so dearly but that other people like a tiny bit less (*What kind of a fucking sadist puts a toe-touch in the middle of cheer for eleven-year-olds?*). Luckily, I am a grown adult who is in full control of her faculties, so after my daughter cries, I tone it the fuck down. I tell her she's doing great. And when she goes to bed, I tell her that I'm pretty sure she'll make the team. She has a kind of luminous quality to her, and she just needs to trust it. My daughter smiles at this. She goes to bed happy.

I believe these words when I say them. But as I close her door, I'm filled with a sense of dread—not because I know what will happen, but because I don't.

"I hate getting invested in something that feels uncertain," I tell Bill as I pour myself a drink. I've tried to avoid overindulging my children. Adaptive animals learn to comfort themselves. But maybe I was only protecting myself from the perils of caring too much.

"Well," he says, choosing his words carefully, which is an extremely wise move at this particular juncture, "it's good that you turned it around." He is referring to how I stopped shouting about my daughter's mistakes and calmed the fuck down. He is referring to my precarious drive right along the edge of unhinged. We both stare at our hands, and I think about how destabilizing it feels to care so much about someone who is not you, particularly when you care about them even more than you care about yourself, when you want the impossible for them, when you'd happily look like Walter Matthau from now on if it meant that that person could feel visible and good and right in their skin starting now until forever. It feels good to care that much, but it also kind of sucks. When the future is out of your control, caring too much can make you feel like a glutton for punishment.

But I don't really want to talk about it.

So now I'm sitting on the couch, wondering if I'm a terrible mother. I wonder if I'll ever say anything right again. That's normal. I love my daughter. I love her much more than I can stand. It hurts sometimes. It's confusing and humbling. That's normal. We're all out of mashed potatoes now.

15

Angry Birds

After you've reached a full decade of marriage, you start to see your mate clearly, free of your own projections and misperceptions. This is not an entirely good thing.

When encountering Bill in our shared habitat, I sometimes experience him as little more than a tangled hill of dirty laundry. "Who left this here?" I ask myself, and then the pile of laundry gets up to fetch himself a cup of coffee. This is not an illusion, it's clarity. Until Bill has enough coffee, he usually lies in an unsightly jumble on the couch, listening to the coffee maker, waiting for it to usher him from the land of the undead. In other words, he is more or less exactly the same as a heap of laundry: smelly, inert, useless, almost sentient but not quite.

Other times I experience Bill as a very handsome professor, a leader among men, a visionary who has big ideas about the future of science education in America. This is clarity. He is all of these things, incredibly enough. And then our dashing hero begins to hold forth on "the learning sciences"—how I hate that term!—and he quickly wilts before my eyes into a cursed academic, a cross between a lonely nerd speaking some archaic language only five other people on earth understand and a haunted ice cream man, circling his truck through the neighborhood in the dead of winter, searching for children. I see Bill with a scorching clarity that pains me.

This is why surviving a marriage requires turning down the volume on your spouse so you can barely hear what they're saying. You must do this not only so you don't overdose on the same stultifying words and phrases within the first year, but also so your spouse's various grunts and sneezes and snorts and throat clearings don't serve as a magic flute that causes you to wander out the front door and into the wilderness, never to return.

When Bill sneezes, it's like a blast from an air horn aimed at your face. No matter where he is in the house, his sneezes are excruciatingly loud. Somehow there are two notes involved, a screechy high one and a shouty low one. It's as if someone in the next room has spotted a bear and they're making this high-pitched yet also bellowing bark of hysteria in order to warn everyone to take cover.

Bill's sneezes are an emergency. I don't think I've ever *not* said "Jesus fucking Christ" out loud upon hearing one. Now that my kids are old enough to register that this horrible sound that's been terrorizing them since they were infants is coming from their father, they join in with their own "Jesus Christs," and then the dogs start barking, and the whole sequence is like an air horn going off, various yelps of panic at the imminent bear attack, and then a chorus of disgusted realizations that this bear will be disrupting our peace until we find some escape route from this godforsaken cave once and for all.

Bill also clears his throat constantly. He's just a phlegmy moth-erfucker in general. I can *almost* get away with being this mean about him because he has remained the same amount of smart and kind and extremely attractive that he was when I met him fifteen years ago. This is just how it feels to be doomed to live and eat and sleep next to the same person until you're dead. Because the resolu-tion on your spouse becomes clearer and clearer by the year, you must find compensatory ways to blur and pixelate them back into a soft, muted, faintly fantastical fog.

It's not easy, though. Because when Bill clears his throat, it's like the fussiest butler in the mansion is about to make a very im-portant announcement and he needs to get the attention of all of the children and wives and animals within earshot. But when you look up from your work, there is no butler there. There is only Bill, staring dumbly at his laptop, with no crucial proclamation forth-coming. Since nagging has zero effect, how do you mute the butler? How do you keep your senses in a defensive stance at all times, ready to preemptively karate-chop the butler before he can blanket you in a sea of phlegmy sound waves?

Do I hate my husband? For sure, yes, definitely. I don't know anyone who's been married more than seven years who flinches at this concept. Before you're married, it's easy to imagine that hating your spouse must mean that you're headed for divorce.

Hating your spouse is as natural as disliking an unexpected bout of the flu. A spouse is a blessing and a curse wrapped into one. How could it be otherwise? How is hatred not the natural outcome of sleeping so close to another human for years, like common criminals? Unless you plug a Propofol drip into your arm every single night, how do you not encounter the grunts and growls and extended gravelly snores of this foul space invader as anything but a pox on your existence? Unless you live inside a virtual reality simulation inhabited by sensitive but seductive half-animal dream lovers during most of your waking hours, how do you not feel the unbearable press of this unruly human in your domicile, rearranging shit but never actually putting it away, opening bills but never actually paying them, shedding his tissues and his terrible droopy cotton boxers and his tiny curly hairs all over your otherwise pristine habitat?

"Well, speak for yourself. *I* don't hate my husband," one of you holier-than-thou marrieds might announce, folding your hands primly in your lap. Do you think I can't see that your left eye is twitching ever so slightly, even as your heart fills with resolve and determination to never, ever allow the little irritations and gentle chafings and burgeoning heaps of contempt add up and move into your conscious mind like a plastic bag floating out to sea and then joining the Great Pacific Garbage Patch?

I admire your mute button. But you can't spend fifteen years with someone who makes as much noise as my husband does and not feel white-hot rage well up inside you occasionally. Yes, of course I also love him. For years, I couldn't imagine a suitable replacement for all of that noise, beyond maybe empty space and blessed silence. Then I started to use my imagination a lot more.

Let's just imagine this: Empty space. Blessed silence. Mmmm, *delicious.*

Because if I'm honest with myself (Bill just hocked back a loogie in the next room), I am too thin-skinned and critical for marriage. I mean, here I am (Bill just coughed and cleared his throat), documenting my husband's flaws in a book, so everyone on earth can read about how disgusting he is, and then I'll feel a tiny bit less alone. I make precise notes about his weaknesses. (Bill just snorted like a prissy bull.) I collect them. It's my hobby.

Do I need to remind you that I'm the villain of this story? Surely not, by now. Surely by now you realize this. I am an actuarial flaw-keeper. I study all of my husband's horrifying quirks and oddities so that I can recast them as comical or delightful inside my head. Is that what I'm doing? Am I building some kind of religion out of a cross between an air horn and a smelly pile of laundry, possibly because I will never remove it from my otherwise peaceful habitat, possibly because I made the mistake of having offspring with this loud heap of nightmares, possibly because I love this cursed ghost?

Or maybe I'm just going to dump the bastard. I would be an idiot to do that, but I can't rule it out.

(Bill is drying his hands quietly. He hasn't made a sound for quite a while.)

(Bill just blew his nose, then gasped, then cleared his throat again.)

Who needs to be cheerful when the plane is delayed by eight hours at midnight? Who speaks calmly when someone sobs uncontrollably as we deboard, even though she doesn't have a plan for where to sleep yet? Who pretends that Doritos and almonds make a fun late dinner at the airport newsstand? Who manages the reservations and the money and the dinner plans through a jet-lagged haze after we land in Sydney? Who books the flights and the ferries and researches the eco-friendly island retreat on the Great Barrier Reef?

Who talks cheerfully through each unpredictable tour through each Australian town full of unpredictable Australian relatives her husband hasn't seen for decades? Who chats amiably with the famous rock star cousin and his girlfriend who is (surprise!) very young, a solid three decades younger than the rock star and more than a decade younger than herself? Who wanders onto the beach, asks the kids what they want to eat, investigates options on Yelp, says order anything, feels queasy, drinks more water, takes photos, makes jokes, tolerates personal slights from her older daughter, engages in the 105th hour of an ongoing discussion about Bill's Bad Knee, which includes speculation, revised imaginary diagnoses, and in-depth analysis of a level of pain that she herself would file under Not Worth Mentioning at All, Ever, Not Even for a Fucking Second?

When we arrive at the island on the Great Barrier Reef, the one populated at this time of year by thousands of birds, birds squawking and cawing and clucking and screeching, birds every two feet, bird shit covering literally every inch of ground, who makes up a game where the first person to get hit by flying bird shit wins an ice cream cone? (You people have no idea how goddamn *good* I am.) Who pulls it together at dinner when the food is so terrible that everyone else is losing it? Who says everyone should get an ice cream cone on the first night regardless, *just because?*

Who says it's okay for one kid not to snorkel? Who says it's okay for both kids to snorkel without her, since she gets seasick? Who goes snorkeling even though she's seasick, because both kids want Mommy to snorkel with them because Daddy will fucking ignore them because he's super jacked up to *snorkel the fuck out of the Great Barrier Reef?* Who asks the snorkeling guide if she might not be better off in the boat since she's starting to get seasick? Who smiles when the snorkeling guide says, in his cavalier Australian-tough-guy accent, that he's not sure *because he's literally never met a human being who got seasick from snorkeling?* Who considers asking the snorkeling dude if he has fucking eyes in his fucking skull since obviously plenty of mortal fucking humans over the age of forty cannot bob on massive fucking swells while looking down fifty feet below them, into a murky shark-filled fucking abyss, and not get a tiny bit dizzy?

Who doesn't say this because it will embarrass her kids and make them call her a Karen? Who vomits straight into the water instead and then watches as dozens of tiny fish swarm up and enjoy *her* breakfast as if it was always intended as *their* breakfast, as if *they* were the ones who stood in line at the shitty fly-covered buffet and listened to the birds squawking everywhere and thought, *Why do people travel at all?*

Okay, then.

And what about the others? One says "I hate this place" the second she sets her feet on the sand. Another says "Why would you do that?" after every single statement made by any other member of her family. And the big one figures out that he lost something and then circles the room like a nervous dog for a solid hour, growling and grumbling and mumbling about the lost thing nonstop, pausing only to hover over whatever you're doing or touch whatever you're touching, pausing to react to every word or action by anyone in the room. He snaps when he hears "Please, just let me do it" and snaps when he hears "Why would you do that?" and snaps when he hears "I hate this." He says "Stop it, stop it, stop it, just stop it!" on a constant loop, morning and night, and nothing will quiet him, and no amount of talking it out will change a thing, and nothing can stop it.

I am reaching my limit. I am outperforming, so goddamn good, every minute of every day, trying so hard to keep everyone together, to keep everyone happy, to make everything better, and I am stuck in an overheated tropical hut with three angry birds that repeat the same words over and over, while a sea of angrier birds outside surrounds us and mocks us. The silver gull cries *I hate this.* The shearwater snipes *Why would you do that?* The buff-sided rail says *Stop it stop it stop it just stop it!*

I have been seasick on and off for a week now. I have a cut on my finger that I'm pretty sure is infected. It was throbbing and red all night. I have been battling raging hormones for over a year. I often feel slightly ill. I can't sleep. I don't say a word about how bad I feel. You don't believe me, but it's true. I have become very good at censoring myself, thanks to writing an advice column for so many years. I have *evolved*, for fuck's sake, unlike my spouse, who has two settings, Asleep and Stop It!

The point is, I am managing myself carefully, unlike the three humans with me. I take strong drugs to prevent further seasickness. I wash the cut. I try to make neutral sounds. You can't be *too* cheerful or everyone gets chippy over how cheerful you are. I try not to react or make sounds at all, unless they are goofy or engaging. I live in the realm of quiet optimism.

This mostly works with the kids, but Bill keeps erasing my efforts with his *stop it stop it.* The kid seems fine but then *stop stop just STOP!* And then that kid is back to, *I hate this I hate this, why would you do that, why why why?*

I shower in the middle of the night to stay cool, I rewash my infected cut, I drink five very small cups of beachy-tasting water to avoid dehydration, I pull my sweater out and drape it across my ears to mute the birds. The birds still sing *I hate this, I hate this, I hate this!* all through the night.

I wake up to the sound of crying from the bed across the room. Trying to quiet this child will only wake up the others, who are sleeping.

Tiny ants are in my drinking cup. A rash guard cannot be located. Someone refuses to shower off, even though it will help with the heat. Someone else announces that she won't snorkel or swim or go anywhere today. I rearrange the beds. I drink my tea. I drink more water. I scrub my clogged, swollen eyelids. I dab acne medicine on my face. I put on sunscreen. The chaotic repeating chorus of kids and parents and birds continues. Everyone in the room is yelling now. The bed sways gently like a raft at sea.

Finally, I break.

"You *all* need to make less noise," I announce to them. "And *you*," I say to the big one, "you're the worst of all. You can't hear a noise without making *another* noise."

At first they're angry. They all start making noises at once. So I raise my voice. "No," I tell them. "I am not the one who fixes things anymore! I am fucking broken! YOU BROKE ME. ARE YOU HAPPY NOW?"

"It's true, but . . ."

"I'm sorry, Mommy."

Now I can't stop. "*Who could stand it?* What kind of a person could hear these fucking noises forever?! Do you know what it takes to hold it together, when you're all doing this shit at the same time? I need a fucking break! Go have breakfast without me!"

My family exits guiltily.

Time alone is better than it used to be. I could never see the benefits before. I can see them clearly now.

∞

Love and hate are intertwined, sometimes to the point where they're almost indistinguishable from each other. I need you, therefore I hate you. I can never leave you, therefore you are my bunkmate in this prison we freely chose, back when we were younger and even stupider than we are now. No sooner are you saved than you start to resent your savior.

Marriage is a solution to several problems that creates infinite additional problems. Marriage can cure your loneliness or exacerbate it. Marriage can make you feel a lot stronger than you really are and a lot weaker than you really are. Marriage can feel like a soothing meditation retreat or a dirty tryst or a very long lunch with the most head-splittingly repetitive human who ever walked the face of the earth. Every week is a little different than the last. Sometimes anger is replaced by indifference. Sometimes anger is replaced by love. Sometimes anger is replaced by outright rage.

After a few days on the island, Bill and I start to tell the kids to walk back to the hotel room after dinner and use their phones for as long as they want. Then we have a drink and stare at the ocean without them. We talk about each kid's breakdown of the day: What did the older one hate today? Which decision did the younger one question? During these conversations, Bill looks handsome to me. He sounds like someone I'm still in love with. The feeling comes back. I understand why I chose him. I understand why we're still together.

But sometimes, when the kids are around, he looks and sounds different. I can appreciate his parenting and his care. I spent years stepping back from trouble and letting him handle it, just so I wasn't the only one. In the beginning, when the kids were babies, I was the one who was always on call. As they got older, I held back so Bill could be the one for some things. On the trip to Australia, I started to see that Bill had become the one for *most* things. He had turned into the mommy, and I hadn't even noticed.

And now I was the dad, more consumed by the thoughts inside my own head, maybe even more ambitious and distracted and restless. I loved being Mommy for years. But now it felt good to be the dad instead. I was more of a dad at heart: arrogant, impatient, discerning about which words came out of my mouth.

But when the shit hit the fan—or when Bill wanted to snorkel without thinking about kids—I was the mom again. Always. I was always on call to step up and do the hardest bits of parenting. When emotions were running high, I would always have to rush in and be the strong, optimistic, helpful one, to save the day.

I couldn't really blame Bill for being the more reactive one. He had less going on inside his head most of the time—that's something he'd freely admit. He was the one who answered most questions. He was also more fixated on discipline and control. Where I saw two kids who were already emotional and high-strung (like their parents) and also very hard on themselves, Bill saw two kids who needed to be herded and reined in and silenced. Their recalcitrance, their open flogging of authority, their questions, their demands, just looked natural to me. As long as they weren't being cruel to us, I felt comfortable hearing their squawking and cawing and clucking and screeching—at home, I did, anyway. I said yes most of the time, and sometimes I said no fucking way and that was it. They didn't ask twice. I indulged them and then sometimes I gave them a look and they knew that they shouldn't push it. When it came to parenting, I had very strong boundaries. My kids seemed to find that more relaxing, even when they weren't getting exactly what they wanted.

Now granted, they always recognized that I was a dormant volcano capable of a much stronger eruption than Bill's smaller, more active volcano, with its highly predictable sputtering and smoking and sparks. I spoke less, but my words carried more authority.

During our drinks at night, I encouraged Bill to be more like me: *Give up control. Relax. Let these birds make their noises, and they'll quiet down quickly. When you treat them like they're doing it wrong, it only gets worse. You need to remember that they're too young to control the sounds they make every second. Step back. Simmer down. Talk yourself off the ledge more, like I do.*

I had learned not to say these things with a condescending or accusatory tone, which would make Bill defensive. He hated to be criticized. He hated even *a whiff* of criticism in the air, at least about important things like child-rearing. I had learned to bide my time and deliver my message over a strong drink. I rarely nagged or snapped now. Over the course of thirteen years of marriage, I had developed the self-control to wait.

But, as you'll recall, Bill doesn't learn new lessons that quickly. He literally studies the learning sciences, which is, let me remind you again, a term that makes me queasy every time I hear it. Yet

after our long discussions on how to manage the kids without losing it, he'd always go right back to saying "Stop it" at the first sign
of tears. And when I heard those kinds of sounds—the repeated,
jackhammery attempts to silence the kids—I lost the handsome
husband. All I could see was the broken robot. All I could hear was
temperamental nonsense and baked-in insecurities and a throat
that clears itself over and over like an old car trying to start up.

I could see Bill clearly, and I was tired of what I was seeing. I
wanted this smelly tangle of laundry to change. For the first time
since we traveled together before we got engaged, I wondered why
a woman should ever spend her life in the company of one man.

It made sense when the kids were little: I needed companionship and support and help. I didn't want to be the only one who
was around all the time, cutting up the apples. But now something
had shifted. It's almost like they needed two mommies now. But
I wasn't sure I wanted to spend my time with another mommy, if
that mommy always sounded the same.

Sometimes I wanted to hear new sounds instead.

∞

When we got back from Australia, I convinced Bill to go back
into therapy. He'd been in therapy years earlier, before we met—
couples therapy with his first wife, then individual therapy as he
was getting separated and divorced. Therapy helped him to decide
that his first marriage was irreparably broken and would never be
fixed. Therapy also helped him to decide that he was *not* irreparably
broken, in spite of believing this for decades. Bill grew up in chaos,

in a house full of siblings that ranged from mildly abusive to indifferent, with two parents who believed you should always keep your feelings to yourself. And when Bill and I met, we got along so well that we somewhat naively figured we'd never need therapy again.

But that year, Bill was grumpy a lot of the time. Meanwhile, I felt happier than I ever had before. I had tried to talk to Bill about his feelings, but it was as if he didn't know how he felt. He would feel fine, and then suddenly he'd get mad over the smallest thing. "You need to figure out how to cultivate an inner life," I'd tell him. He'd agree, and then he'd go back to feeling weirdly empty and lost after that. We knew the pattern, but at some point it seemed like it was out of my control. Besides, I felt like I had enough on my plate, between kids and dogs and books and column deadlines. It was time for my loud, grouchy husband to go make noises to some extremely compassionate professional and leave me in peace for a change.

Here I will admit that I was also a tiny bit worried that if Bill got enough therapy, he would start spraying his feelings all over the place like a healthy person. A tiny part of me wanted him to remain out of touch with himself. I wasn't sure that our marriage had room for two vulnerable, emotional beings.

This worry was counterbalanced by another worry: that Bill would review my alternately avoidant and self-obsessed and relentlessly critical behavior over the past thirteen years of marriage and conclude that I was a bad person and leave me. I didn't think there was a high probability of this happening, but the thought did cross my mind. I mean, he was a man, after all. Men are often shut down and confused and dumb that way, aren't they?

He would start feeling his feelings and then he'd fall in love with his therapist or some sexy younger colleague and he'd leave me in the dust. Some days he'd come home and tell me something smart that his therapist told him, and I'd have trouble not saying, "I've literally said that to you a million times, you know that, right?" I would bite my tongue, remembering that Bill was handsome and could simply begin fucking this brilliant therapist without remembering that all of her best ideas had been foreshadowed by his wife for thirteen years.

When I thought about Bill's brilliant therapist, I sometimes worried that she might be beautiful in addition to being insightful about Bill's troubles. Was I beautiful, though? I had always experienced myself as not quite attractive enough. Bill claimed that I was hot, but when I looked in the mirror that year, what I saw was a very harried, graying woman who was arguably past her prime. She also seemed creepily confident in herself, considering these things. Perhaps she was wildly deluded about her quality as a person, thanks to the consistently loving husband who was about to leave her for someone much better.

On the other hand, I was so happy and so fit! I walked six miles on my treadmill desk almost every day and I was more productive than ever and I had lots of new writer friends, too. I loved my career and I was a decent mother and I know this is hard to believe at this particular juncture but I *was* very very fun to be around! Ask my kids! I was fun!

It would be easy for Bill to convince his brand-new lover— colleague or therapist, whoever!—that I was a fucking shrew, nevertheless. *Any* husband can convince a random woman that his wife is awful, if he wants to. That's how you unlock the next-level sex with your future third wife: you tell her all about how much your second wife sucks. Maybe in the future Bill can save himself a lot of time and effort and just hand his future third wife this book and say, "It's all in there."

So I resolved to listen patiently to Bill whenever he wanted to talk about his feelings or talk about therapy. I needed to be on my best behavior while he was feeling fragile and hopeful and full of invigorating fear and possibilities. I want you to notice that this felt a little foreign and exotic to me, at that time. I was happy, but I was a tiny bit withdrawn from my marriage. It is possible—easy, in fact—to be both.

Bill and I started to go on long walks with the dogs together around then. Bill was on sabbatical that spring, so we had the time. We also had a new puppy named Fig that was going through an insecure phase, and our older but smaller dog, Olive, had learned a lot of bad habits from her very dominant older sister, Potus, now deceased. In the old days, Potus would stare down rival dogs until they were in a state of murderous rage, and then our little dog Olive would go nuts, barking and snipping and twisting around on her leash in a state of panic.

Then Potus died and we threw a big, easily threatened puppy into the mix. Now we had two very insecure dogs prone to panicking on walks. Panicking dogs look a lot like panicking children. They spin in circles and bark furiously and bite each other's faces. Panicking dogs sound a lot like angry birds, except they can sink their teeth into your ankles and then you'll need some antibiotics and a tetanus shot.

And as was true with our other angry birds, negative reinforcement was not that effective. Yanking on their leashes and saying "No!" worked reasonably well with our overconfident alpha dog.

For these two insecure dogs, it just added to the chaos. These dogs needed a calm, confident master.

So I read a book about positive reinforcement clicker training, I tried it out on the dogs, and I taught it to Bill. Bill did not read the book. Bill did not understand clicker training. And Bill would not have purchased the book and learned its ways or even tried to solve the problem at all. In our marriage and in our house, I was the problem solver. I was also the visionary. Bill was the middle manager, with all of the positive and negative connotations that implies.

Neither one of us could walk both nervous, agitated dogs alone. So we walked the dogs together every day.

At first, we still had trouble talking for a full hour every day. It wasn't that we didn't talk to each other a lot. We grappled with concrete managerial concerns around the kids and the house and the dogs every day, and we also had longer, sweeping conversations about how we felt and what we wanted from our jobs and anything else, at night and during the day when Bill wasn't teaching or meeting with grad students or whatever other boring things he did at work. But I wanted our walks to be about therapy and ideas and things that interested me, and I did not want to talk about Bill's work. No fucking way.

I need for you to understand how uninteresting I find Bill's job. It's one of my major flaws as a spouse that I have never found any real connection to Bill's area of study or to research in the social sciences or to university life in general. It all sounds so dull to me, and that's never changed. Bill is also a shitty storyteller when it comes to anything work-related. I mean human drama and conflict with coworkers are at least mildly enjoyable topics, but sadly, with Bill, even the most dramatic stories are bookended with state-ments like "See, the Center for Blarga Blarga is investigating new pathways into various learning sciences technologies, with the understanding that any technologies will have to be implemented in ways that underscore the student's self-directed discovery of tools that might better enable self-directed, discovery-based learning, so they're calling for papers on these technologies under the guise of . . ." Even that sentence is far more interesting and dynamic than the sentence that might come out of Bill's face. It's more interesting and dynamic *because I wrote it*, and also because I am more interesting and dynamic than Bill. It's true, ask anyone.

I'm also a much bigger asshole than he is.

Which is the real point to our story. Because as we're walking, Bill and I start talking more and more about Bill's experiences in therapy. And Bill basically tells me that he doesn't want to go too deep into the darkness because he's afraid he might just turn into a pile of nerves and bones and mush and he'll be a big emotional mess and I'll decide that he's unlovable. And I keep saying to Bill, "Dude, remaining disordered and confused and reactionary is what's unlovable. *Darkness* is not unlovable. *Falling apart* is not unlovable. I *love* vulnerability and weakness." I mean, this is what I do, right? I'm an advice columnist, and I'm goddamn poetic when it comes to the subject of darkness and fear and vulnerability. It's my thing!

Now cut to Bill, on the couch, crying, exactly as I urged him to do, while I pat him on the head. Am I thinking, *This is what it's all about, I love this expressive, vulnerable man?*

No. I'm thinking, *I might spend the rest of my life doing this.*

There are sounds you make when you start therapy. Everyone

makes them. No matter how good your childhood might have been, when you start therapy, you recognize what you didn't get from your childhood, from your parents, from your family life, from your first days on the planet. You suddenly recognize what was missing. Unfortunately, this process sounds self-pitying at first. That's just the nature of the process. And to Bill's credit, he didn't fill an entire memoir with these sounds the way I did.

So zoom in on Bill, a very good person who is feeling his feelings as directed by his wife. Bill grew up being told, literally, "No one wants to hear about your feelings!" Bill grew up feeling invisible. Let me offer you an image that will crush your heart: Bill's eyes were crossed at birth, and it took years until his parents finally had them fixed. And then Bill had to have glasses—he needed them to see. But one day Bill lost his glasses. Bill's mom, who was a very good mother in many ways, was also very tough. Their vision plan only covered one pair of glasses a year, so she told him, "Looks like you'll have to wait until next year to get new glasses." Bill walked around not being able to see for a whole year. It was awful.

And then, when Bill finally got glasses again, everyone at school called him four eyes and told him he was a nerd. He'd never felt like a nerd before. He'd been walking around with crossed eyes, feeling happy and fine, and now it was like he'd eaten fruit from the forbidden tree and his innocence was gone! But when he went to his mom and tried to explain how hard things were, she scolded him and told him to stop complaining.

So now you can imagine Bill feeling sad. Of course he feels sad! He had a mom who was very kind, but she was utterly indifferent to his emotions. Then he had a first wife who was also pretty indifferent. He felt sorry for himself! Half a lifetime of indifference! Who wouldn't feel sorry for themselves?

Now zoom in on me, the second wife, patting his head while he cries, thinking, *I can't do this forever. This could break me.*

I was the one who told him to walk straight into the darkness, and now I felt cold! My total lack of empathy was shocking to me in that moment. It made me feel sick inside. It made me feel guilty.

I couldn't let it go. I felt so terrible about it. It was like this huge sin that I needed to confess, just to stop feeling so ill. So later, we're lying in bed and Bill is cuddling up to me and saying he feels so grateful for me and so grateful for us. He's telling me that crying made him feel *so* much better. He is still very attractive, mind you, and his breath doesn't *even* smell bad at the moment. *He* feels very close to me now. This is what I wanted.

But I am not feeling that close to him. I'm not at my best late at night. And I'm not at my best when a grown adult needs me, sometimes. Children? Easy. But a grown man? Horrific! I guess I'm a little sexist. And sometimes when you used to be emotionally insecure and you've found your way out of that mess, your underlying shame gives you a slight *aversion* to neediness.

Or maybe I've been a parent for so long that I'm a little bit tired of giving. I just want to be the grumbly dad who reads the paper and tosses back a drink and drops off into a deep sleep.

I'm in a weird phase. But I can't lie to Bill. That's one unfortunate fact that will become increasingly clear as our story progresses. I know that if I lie about how I feel, it will turn me against him. I spent decades doing that. My lying about my needs and feelings turned me against a whole sea of people.

So I tell Bill about my lack of empathy. I tell him, basically, *In that moment that I was stroking your hair and you were crying, I did not feel close to you. I felt distant.*

Bill immediately gets mad. I'd be mad too.

"I'm not saying that I don't *want* you to cry," I tell him. "I'm not saying that I'll always be disgusted with you when you cry. I'm feeling disgusted with myself. That's what I'm saying. I'm telling you something vulnerable and embarrassing. I'm *embarrassed* by what a fucking asshole I am."

And then I start to cry, and he pats me on the head and probably also feels a lack of empathy for me, equal and opposite to my own.

"But this is how I stay," I tell Bill. "By telling the whole truth. I don't want to close my heart to you. I *want* to feel close to you. The only way I know how to feel close to you is by telling you what a shriveled-up rotten heart I have sometimes. That's my darkness. I can't pretend it's not there, or I'll lose you. We'll lose each other. I want you to see the real me. I need to see the real you. That's how we'll stay together."

Bill isn't a good learner, but he is a good listener. He understood. Honesty was our only path forward. Neither of us could control our emotions. All we could do was tell each other the truth.

I felt close to Bill after that. We both felt closer.

I didn't believe that our marriage was on the line that night, as we talked it all out and then told each other we loved each other and then felt proud of how much we dared to talk about. I didn't actually think our marriage was the subject of conversation when we walked for an hour every day for eight months straight. I didn't think that we were renegotiating ways of moving through the world together. I didn't think we were finally getting on the same page so thoroughly that we could also, finally, maybe, wander off that page without worrying about it too much.

I didn't think I had anything to worry about. I knew, in my heart, that we would be together forever, thanks to our honesty. That didn't sound bad to me. It sounded just right.

I didn't know how much that feeling was about to change.

PART IV

16

Crushed

In the spring of 2019, a well-known author I'd met at a book festival invited me out to dinner at a nice restaurant in Silver Lake with a handful of other writers and journalists. I'd liked the guy from the moment I met him a year earlier. He had a blasé confidence that yielded unexpectedly to goofy enthusiasm, like a little boy dressed up in his father's suit. The first time we met, he said something self-deprecating and forlorn out of the blue, and a twisted voice inside my head whispered, *This guy needs you.*

That was unusual, but I didn't overthink it at the time. When his email appeared out of the blue, I felt flattered and also excited to put on lipstick and hang out with new people instead of slumping on the couch in my soft pants, watching *Parks and Recreation* with the kids for the fifty thousandth night in a row.

When I got to the restaurant, I sat at the bar and had a cocktail by myself. After a few minutes the author appeared, and he was exactly as I remembered him: funny, a little awkward, very boyish. He sat down next to me and ordered a drink. Then, one by one, the other guests showed up and introduced themselves.

Sometime during the first course, I realized I was having the best time I'd had in months. These were the kinds of people—combative nerds with way too many opinions—I used to hang out with around the clock before I got married. This was the sort of conversation—funny and fast-paced, mixing current events with theories and gossip—that I never had in the suburbs. We bounced from one idea to the next, laughing, swearing, rolling our eyes, getting a little obnoxious. I was free to be my aggressive self without setting anyone's teeth on edge.

Sometime during the main course, I realized that it had been years since I'd been around men other than Bill who actually seemed to be listening to what I was saying. The dads in the suburbs were perfectly fine, but except for one guy friend, a therapist with a dark sense of humor, most of them talked to me like I was an obstacle to navigate around. To be fair, I treated them the same way. I'd encounter them mumbling and chuckling with each other on the elementary school grounds, dressed in cargo shorts and basketball sneakers just like their kids, and I'd bypass their slouching frames without thinking twice.

Bill and I hosted casual parties frequently, but nothing fun or interesting ever seemed to happen. Every discussion among other parents circled around marriage or kids or the latest news, taking the soggy shape of a bad book-club conversation: hopelessly tentative, polite, and evasive, with everyone working hard to say as little as possible. Even heated arguments among my oldest friends who lived in other neighborhoods lost steam quickly, replaced by early departures or strumming guitars around a campfire for hours on end. Kids' activities always took precedence over adult conversations. I met friends for one-on-one dinners out, but that never had the same energy as a boisterous group.

Sometimes it felt like my head was teeming with thoughts and opinions that no one wanted to hear anymore. And like a parent holding up a baby in a pool and mimicking dog paddling until the baby is convinced she can swim, Bill treated every word out of my mouth like it was interesting and worthwhile, until I believed it, too. Then I went out into the world and sank like a stone.

But not that night. Sometime during dessert, I realized the author who'd invited me and the handsome journalist sitting to my right were both listening closely to every word I said. It was almost like they were competing for my attention. My advice column was pro-love but firmly against trying to figure out what shape to take to please a man. "Take a bossy, inconvenient shape and see who likes *that*," I often wrote. And now I was being bossy out in the wild, and no one was backing away.

Right before the check came, someone's foot was suddenly resting on my ankle. I slowly moved my foot away. A minute later, the foot returned. *What the fuck?* I moved my foot under my chair, feeling a little anxious. I could see out of the corner of my eye that the author was leaning way back in his chair, as if stretching to reach my feet.

A minute later, the foot rested very firmly on my ankle, which was fully tucked under my chair by then. I jumped a little and quickly jerked away, feeling panicked. *Are you kidding me?*

After dinner, the author and the journalist and I stood in front of the restaurant chatting about nothing. The author asked for a ride to his hotel, which was on my way home. *This will be awkward,* I thought. *But interesting!*

In the car, we talked about his work, my work. Wasn't he going to bring it up? He said something about how we're all "trying to feel more," and I wondered if that was the point of the foot thing. I figured he was about to explain himself, but when we got to the busy corner next to his hotel, he jumped out of my car, barely saying goodbye. *He must be embarrassed,* I thought, watching him cross the street in front of my car, looking self-conscious. *He wants to pretend it never happened.* I texted Bill, "On my way. Stay awake!"

By the time I got home, I was a proud cat with a dead bird. "Guess what?" I said, picking up my toothbrush. "The author guy hit on me! He put his foot on my foot, under the table."

"Weird!" Bill put down his iPad and looked at me. "But it was probably a mistake."

"It happened three times!" I burbled through my toothbrush. "*Definitely* not a mistake."

"Oh my god. Isn't he married?"

"Yeah! Do you think famous writers do this all the time? They just run around kicking people and taking them back to their hotel rooms?"

"Maybe. But it seems risky. What was he thinking?"

"I don't know!" I climbed into bed, grinning. "Maybe he thought I was coming on to him."

Bill turned toward me with his head propped up on his elbow. "So, you *want* to fuck this guy?"

"No way! Gross!" I said, rubbing Bill's arm. "I mean, I *like* him. He's cute."

Bill was already googling the author on his phone. "He looks like a chubby cop from Cleveland."

"Yeah, but he's still cute," I said. "And chubby is kind of my type. Or it used to be."

"So you'd fuck him."

"Ha ha, *no*. No way."

Kissing him wouldn't be so bad, I thought, guiltily. Particularly if he made some big confession of love . . . or not love, because that would be delusional. *Obsession*, maybe. If he said "I've been thinking about you ever since we met," and *then* we kissed? The thrill of that would be hard to resist.

But actually having sex? Getting naked and rubbing your body all over a stranger's body? Jesus. That was like something you saw at the Monterey Bay Aquarium.

So Bill and I joked about how absurd it was that this idiot thought I wanted him, and I felt high from my dinner, high from the miracle that anyone found me attractive, high from being obnoxious around people who actually enjoyed it. That was how I'd spent college and my early twenties: verbally sparring with men, making sweeping proclamations, showing off. I'd written off those years as a kind of haze of douchiness, but wasn't that part of my personality? Didn't I thrive among outspoken, swaggery geeks? Didn't I miss it a little?

We talked for a while, and then we made out, and it was hot. It was nothing like Monterey Aquarium.

∞

The next morning, Bill was packing his suitcase for a conference on the East Coast when I woke up. "Are you gonna call your cop buddy and invite him over?" he asked. "He might still be in town."

"Oh, definitely," I said, putting down my book. "I'll tell the kids 'Mommy's new boyfriend is here.' They won't like him at first, but they'll adjust eventually."

We kissed goodbye and I lay back in bed, listening to the front door open and then close with a thud. Now Bill got to get on a plane and go somewhere, and I was at home, as usual. My life was beyond boring. And the cute author guy also got to fly all over the world, playing footsie with random women, maybe having sex with some of them. How did he get away with it?

I imagined him in nice hotel rooms in Italy, in London, in Dubai, fucking a new woman in every city. Could he pull it off? He wasn't an Adonis, but he was charming and funny and he had a nice smile. I could see it working. He seemed harmless. That probably worked to his advantage.

I couldn't quite picture his face, though. I tried to imagine it, but it was a blur. Was it *actually* cute, or was it just your average dumb dad face? I googled his name and found some dumb dad pictures. And then I found an interview.

In the interview, the author was defending a hot take he'd written. The interviewer was firing challenging questions at him. The author wasn't smiling the way I remembered him smiling. His eyes were small and mean. The interviewer would try to throw him off guard or get him to admit he was wrong, but the author wouldn't budge an inch.

Something shifted under my skin. The author wasn't harmless.

He wasn't even that nerdy. And he wasn't just opinionated, he was arrogant. How did I miss this completely?

I watched the interview again. He was also smarter than I remembered.

I watched the interview again, hating myself for it. This guy was flying all over the place, my husband was flying all over, and I was reduced to sitting around in bed, thinking about how nice it would be to fly somewhere for a change, to stay in an expensive hotel room and have sex with some completely indifferent cheater with dirty cheating eyes and a mean little cheating face. I thought about his wife at home, waiting for him, probably bored out of her skull, too. That made me feel guilty. *But maybe she's done with him,* I thought. *Maybe they have an open marriage. Maybe they're staying together for the kids.*

I watched the interview again. This man was stupidly sexy. It almost made me mad, how sexy he was.

$$\infty$$

When Bill called me from his hotel on the East Coast the next morning, I was drinking my tea and staring out at the swaying bamboo fronds in the backyard, but my mind was packed full of 1990s-suspense-thriller-style hotel room sex: on the sink, in the closet, against the wall.

"I feel really guilty, baby," I whispered into the phone, even though the kids were upstairs playing Mario Kart with the door closed. "I looked up all of these interviews with that author, and they were actually really impressive and he looked pretty hot and I started imagining having sex with him and it doesn't seem bad and gross anymore, not at all. It seems fun and exciting now."

"So, you actually want to sleep with that dude?"

"Not in real life! I've just been . . . picturing it a lot. It's stuck on a loop in my head. And now I'm confessing it to you, like Jimmy fucking Carter!"

"Do you feel dissatisfied? Should I be worried?"

"No, of course not. But *cheating in general* suddenly sounds like the best thing ever. Fucking someone you barely know in a nice hotel room somewhere? And you're sneaking around and lying about it? Plus there's no time, and you'll never be there again? I finally get it. And I'll never get to do it."

"Oh poor you, you have a good marriage so you can't cheat."

"I know, it's dumb. I'm sorry."

"You don't have to apologize just for imagining things. Haven't you ever fantasized about anyone before?"

"Not since before we were married." Picturing sex with other men had always felt like cheating to me, a bad mental habit that could only lead to danger. Now danger sounded perfect.

"Cheating is never as simple as you imagine," Bill said. "Someone always gets hurt." He'd had affairs during his previous marriage, which was *almost* open—more like *ajar*, as if the latch on the door was broken and no one had bothered to fix it.

I'd had lots of one-night stands when I was younger, but they always seemed sordid in retrospect. I thought I'd gotten that out of my system. Besides, I never liked being single that much, didn't love dating, never tolerated hanging out and hooking up without a commitment, and disliked uncertainty in general. I had always just wanted to find my person and be done with it.

But now that I was a grown adult woman who had learned to love her body, who felt fully present and unashamed in the right company, my concept of what was possible had shifted without warning. It suddenly seemed feasible to have a one-night stand (or even a brief affair, preferably on some tropical island in the middle of the ocean!), and it would just be a big fat bonus added on to my preexisting life, kind of like second breakfasts in *The Hobbit*.

"Maybe we could each get a side piece or whatever." I knew Bill wouldn't go for it. We had friends who were swingers and even though I never liked the sound of that life, I *did* want to hear their stories in detail, whereas Bill just found them depressing. "We could agree to go on a vacation with someone else once a year, and we'd come back refreshed and inspired."

"Is that really what you want?" Bill said. "Because all I can think about is the drawbacks."

"Whatever, I'm just spitballing!" I said, watching the fronds of my papyrus plant sway in the wind.

"*We* need to go on a vacation by ourselves," Bill said.

"Yeah, we do." That sounded good, too, but not quite as thrilling.

∞

By the time Bill got back to town, the new lingerie I'd ordered had already arrived. For years I'd been sleeping in what might be politely described as extremely lightweight short pajamas, but would more accurately be described as threadbare rags. The shift to lacy nighties was abrupt. Bill couldn't believe his luck. I'd become the cheesy protagonist of a *Cosmo* story on spicing up your married sex life.

I didn't care. I told myself I was entering a new phase of shamelessness. I had tons of energy from walking on my treadmill every day, and I was happier than ever. The kids were big enough to be occupied with school and friends. Bill had taken over a lot of cooking and housework while he was on sabbatical. I had more time and freedom than I'd had since before I had kids. I felt younger than I had in years.

Every morning I woke up early to write, feeling expansive and optimistic. I would listen to Beethoven's symphonies and write wild prose for my newsletter. All of the bad noises and worries and fears that used to run my life were suddenly gone, and I was free to enjoy myself and follow my whims wherever they led.

One afternoon, after spontaneously making out in the upstairs bedroom, I told Bill, "I feel like a man. Predatory. Like I want to track animals across the snowy wilderness."

"You sound like a teenage boy."

"Yeah, that's how I feel! I feel like my body's been asleep, like I didn't even know how to pay attention to it until now." I raised my bare feet and legs into the air and stared at them. "I wonder how long this will last? I don't want it to end."

"Neither do I."

Birds were singing outside. I stared at the square of blue sky visible through the window and thought about the friends I knew who were getting divorced, and the friends who weren't having sex anymore but *weren't* getting divorced. We were pretty lucky.

I pictured the author and his wife in Seattle. Were they good together? Were they unhappy? Did he cheat on her even when he was in town?

Bill sat up to put on his shirt. *My husband is extremely hot*, I thought.

Bill picked up his phone and stared at it.

I wonder what my imaginary boyfriend is doing right now.

∞

That fall, I flew to Seattle for a book event. The last night I was in town, I was supposed to have a drink with a friend, but she bailed on me at the last minute. So I walked back to my hotel and considered going up to the rooftop bar for a drink by myself.

I'd thought about getting in touch with the author to hang out, but I was worried that he'd think I wanted to sleep with him, so I decided not to. I didn't completely trust myself not to do something stupid. But now I was thinking, *I should've texted him.* Sitting across from him, sipping a cocktail in the chill of early autumn, sounded like the perfect way to end my trip.

In person, I could finally ask him, *What was that foot thing about? Is that just a thing you do? How do you justify it to yourself?*

I unlocked my hotel room, fished my phone out of my bag, and lay down on the bed. *I can't text him now*, I thought. *It'll look like a booty call.*

I pictured Bill at home, playing his stupid golf game in bed, and felt guilty. *Being married is like being a teenager with a curfew*, I thought. *You're never really free. You're always tied to someone else. I wish I could make my own choices without worrying about how they'll affect Bill.*

I got up from the bed and sifted idly through the tasteful little packages of cashews and wasabi peas and pretty bottles of craft gin and bourbon. *We wouldn't have to do anything. Just talking about attraction over a good drink would be the most erotic thing ever.*

It was all perfectly safe. He clearly didn't want to burn his life to the ground, and neither did I. He would never get hung up on me, so I'd never have to feel bad about anything. Plus, he was already fucking around. I wouldn't be the cause of his downfall. And once I got him talking, he would tell me all of his secrets, like everyone does.

Mmm, secrets. I walked into the bathroom and stared at my face in the mirror. *But maybe he was never that attracted to me in the first place. Even mentioning it might creep him out. Maybe he was just being reckless, and I just happened to be there.*

Somehow the author's interest felt like a verdict on my value in the world. I knew that was stupid, but I couldn't shake it. How much longer would I have the sex drive of a teenage boy? How long would I even be alive at all? All of the possibilities in the world felt like they were narrowing.

$$\infty$$

After that night, the author moved into my head permanently. We would exchange polite emails every few months, but he never pushed any boundaries, so it felt unethical to push any myself. I complimented him a little too much. I was a tiny bit flirtatious. But I felt dumb whenever I did those things, so mostly I stayed silent.

Instead, I tried to solve the mystery of who he was and what he wanted just by thinking about it constantly. It was my new cognitive hobby. I started analyzing his most meaningless emails for subtext. Was he flirting? Mocking me? Pitying me? Breadcrumbing? Did he have an open marriage? As an advice columnist, I was used to people telling me everything. This was a completely unfamiliar experience. The man was a locked door. I studied his tweets, loomed around his Instagram account, analyzed his follow list, but only found the most meager clues about who he was and what he wanted. I felt like I was struggling to jimmy a lock that wouldn't budge. *I just want information*, I told myself. *That's natural. I'm not being creepy. I haven't done anything.* But I felt like an asshole for caring so much about something so small and stupid.

And I felt guilty about his wife, so I kept telling myself that she was probably gay or their marriage was open or both. It was ludicrous but the more I imagined it, the more real it seemed.

Bill seemed more bored by talk of my crush than worried about it. But privately, *I* was a little worried. Bill and I had talked before about how we wouldn't leave each other just for cheating, as long as it wasn't embedded in a web of lies. But who knew what he'd really do if I went for it?

"You'd feel too weird," Bill said one morning when I brought it up on our walk. The sky was overcast and the air was chilly, so we were walking faster than usual.

"Maybe. But I'm thinking about it way too much. I could have sex with SpongeBob SquarePants if I thought about him *this* much."

"So why don't you stop?" Bill looked confused.

"Believe me, I've tried." He was being so nice. It made me want to push it a little. "Maybe I should just fuck the guy and get it out of my system once and for all."

"Are you trying to ask for permission? Because you have to make your own choices. It has nothing to do with me."

"But I'd never do anything without your permission," I said. "I'd feel too guilty."

"Don't worry about how I'll feel. Worry about how *you'll* feel."

This wasn't exactly permission, but some monstrous part of my brain thought, *Oh goody! Now I get to do whatever I want!*

∞

A few months later, the author emailed to tell me he'd be visiting town and we should hang out. I was ecstatic! I couldn't wait to make out with my brand-new lover whose wife was for sure definitely gay, 100 percent the gayest and not even curious about where her husband was or what he was doing!

The day before we were supposed to meet, the author emailed me and suggested lunch. Ugh! My brand-new married boyfriend was not into me at all. I was too old and gross! He had fifteen other mistresses around the world, and I didn't make the cut.

The next day, his plans changed, and he asked if we could meet for a drink instead. Yesss! My new lover was dying to see me, so he could finally tell me how unbelievably irresistible I was in person. *You can never leave a paper trail*, he'd explain. *Goddamn, you look good.*

I spent a long time making my hair and makeup just right. *Everything's going to be fine*, I told myself. *We'll make out and it'll be thrilling and then I'll come home. Who cares? People do it every day. No big deal.* It was going to be wild to kiss someone new after thirteen years! Wheeeee!

Bill was still miraculously unconcerned. His attitude toward the author had remained condescending but tolerant. Sometimes he'd call him "the round guy" or "that chubby cop you love so much," like the author was my mostly harmless imaginary friend.

I was putting on lipstick when Bill came in the bedroom. I needed to leave soon to make it downtown in time, but seeing him made me feel self-conscious.

"You look nice," he said. "I hope your little buddy likes it."

"Do you think I should bail?" This was a bluff. There was no fucking way I was going to bail.

"No," Bill said. "Go find out what his story is. When will you have another chance?"

The bar where we agreed to meet was very rich-mature-adult in a bad way, with brass and leather booths and TV screens everywhere. But when I spotted the author at the bar, I felt a rush of affection for him. He was such an odd mix of guarded and unguarded, professional and childlike: his cute smile, his weird low voice that cracked a lot, his stubby little bear paws. He waved hello without making any move to get up from his chair or kiss my cheek, but then we quickly fell into chatting about writer things. He was exceedingly polite. His teeth were a little weird. The collar of his shirt was a tiny bit too tight. I had to admit, it was very hard to imagine kissing him. Not Monterey Aquarium hard, but not easy. How would we even *get* there?

I ordered a Last Word and he gamely ordered the same thing. *That's what I like about this guy,* I thought. *He's arrogant, but he still knows how to follow a woman's lead.* Sipping from our tiny coupe glasses, we talked about writers we liked, writers we disliked, people we knew in common. The author was very funny, a little sly, and a little distracted, too. He checked his phone at one point, and I found myself thinking, *He's kind of jumpy. He needs someone to show him how to stay present.*

I did want to kiss him.

But he really wasn't bringing the same vibe to the table. He didn't seem that interested, and he definitely wasn't obsessed. He didn't even seem . . . familiar with me, somehow? How was that possible? Was he playing it off?

We were about to pay the bill, and finally I turned to him. This was my last chance. If I didn't say something now, I'd have to wait another year, two years, who knew how long?

I took a deep breath and turned to him. "Do you dislike . . . directly addressing things that are . . . in the room?"

"No. What do you mean?" He looked genuinely confused.

"But you don't really like to . . . address the *obvious* thing."

"Huh?"

"Okay, so maybe I should ask *Greg* if he kicked me under the table that night we had dinner." Greg was married and had been too far away to reach me, plus I'm pretty sure he won Least Likely to Play Footsy with a Stranger in high school.

"Greg?" the author asked, blinking at me confusedly.

"Or maybe I should ask *Jack* if he kicked me." Jack was the handsome guy sitting to my right that night, but this was also a joke. Jack was way out of my league and a solid decade younger than me.

"Jack kicked you under the table that night?" The author's face dropped like he was shocked.

Suddenly I had a flashback, like something out of a cartoon: the foot always came from the right side of me. But Jack had never even occurred to me! I'd just met Jack. I didn't know him at all.

My face felt hot. I looked at my imaginary boyfriend, and I could tell he wasn't lying. *He never fucking touched me.* I'd been fantasizing about someone who never even thought of me at all.

The author and I stared at each other. We were both smiling now, saying nothing. "This is *Fleabag*," I said, finally. "I am starring in an episode of *Fleabag*."

I put my head down on the bar.

"Don't feel bad," the author said.

"Mother*fucker*! This is . . . *mortifying*."

"I can kick you now, if that helps." The author felt sorry for me. I felt like screaming,

When I got to my car, I did scream. Then I called Bill. "You're not going to *FUCKING* believe this." I told him the story. I screamed "Fuuuuuuck!" at least five times. "Can you believe it?" I kept saying. "Can you *fucking believe it?*"

When I got home, we made out. Afterward, we lay in bed, side by side, staring at the ceiling.

"I am such an idiot," I said.

"Well, it's over now," Bill said. "No harm done."

$$\infty$$

But the next morning, it didn't seem funny anymore. I wanted to feel relieved—at least now I won't accidentally fuck my life into the ground!—but instead I just felt sad. The author was just another dad man in cargo shorts, mumbling on the schoolyard and distractedly navigating around me. And I was deluded and sick—a foolish, very bad person. There weren't any adventures to be had. The world was smaller and less interesting than I'd thought it was.

"Why does it matter?" Bill asked me when I tried to explain why I felt so let down. "The hot guy hit on you. It's not like *nothing* happened." That did help. It also helped that my husband was willing to chat about the whole thing like we were two teenagers lying on our canopy beds and gossiping into our princess phones.

But I still felt disappointed. I didn't even know Jack. He was single and probably hit on me on a whim. There was no lock to jimmy open. My author crush was the puzzle I wanted to solve, but there was no puzzle there, either. I wanted my chubby cop boyfriend back!

"Why do you care about this so much?" Bill asked.

"I don't know!" The question alone made me pathetic. "Because . . . because I'm *old!*" I said, bursting into tears. "I'm old and you're old and nothing new is ever going to happen to us! We're going to die soon and we'll never do anything exciting or weird or crazy before then. We'll just get older and older and everything will stay exactly the same until we're dead."

I was right that death was closer than we thought. But I was wrong that nothing would ever change. Everything was about to go haywire.

17

Pestilence

For months after that, I felt like a jackass about the comedy of errors I'd invited into the center of our life. Bill and I thoroughly metabolized every dimension of the situation together (yeah, poor Bill), but it definitely brought us closer, and it loosened up our ideas about how we should be living. Bill started to talk more about the things he wanted to do—golfing and going on golf trips, mostly—that didn't interest me that much. And I started to rethink how I'd been living for years: working from home, going out one night a week for an early dinner with a friend, throwing parties for suburban parents, but just generally feeling pretty bored and disappointed with my social life.

So we resolved to have more adventures, together and apart. I needed to get out of the house more, gather some combative nerds around me, make new connections, explore the world after a long era of living the life of the work-from-home, domesticated shut-in. I was filled with a sense that we didn't have much time to live exactly the way we wanted to live, so we needed to go for it immediately.

First we visited Hawaii over Christmas with my mom and my sister and her family, an enormous extravagance that we could hardly afford, but it was the most relaxing, deeply satisfying vacation I'd ever taken. When we got back, I started to make plans with friends, new and old. I rented an office in Silver Lake so I could get out of the house several days a week and meet people after work for drinks or dinner. I planned an apocalypse-themed party for local writers the night after Valentine's Day, because, between climate change, Trump's accelerating madness, and the virus ravaging China, it felt like the world was ending.

Bill encouraged me to spend more time away from home. He'd been driving across town to teach and meet with colleagues for years. He traveled alone for work often and loved it. He was glad to see that I'd found a way to become more social without going completely off the deep end and flying to an island in the middle of the Pacific to solve a cop-shaped puzzle with my naked body.

I mostly gave up my cognitive crushing hobby. Other men would DM me on Twitter after reading something vulnerable or unhinged I'd written in my column or my newsletter, but none of them had the total lack of interest in sharing their secrets with me that was apparently necessary to transform me into Pepé Le Pew. Sometimes I still wished I could have a *real* crush, one that could indefinitely fuel my most fantastical thoughts and keep me writing evocative prose about chasing prey across the snowy wilderness. But I started to find that I could conjure that feeling without needing a target to inspire me. It was just a matter of savoring my desires, believing in my longing, and celebrating my unexpected evolution into an openly intense superfreak.

So even though the crush ended in 1980s-sitcom-style humiliation, I resolved to keep the parts of that experience that I liked
(new connections, imaginative leaps, occasional bouts of shamelessness) and lose the rest (creepiness, oversharing, building an al-
ternative reality inside my head). Life *should* be intense. Friends
should feel deeply connected to each other. And I *should* be able to
befriend people of any gender without feeling weird or guilty or as-
suming it'll lead to something more.

In some ways, the crush was an echo of my hunger for a deeper
connection—to my friends, to Bill, to my family. But I also wanted
to belong to myself again. I wanted Bill to have more freedom, too.
The main focus of our lives shouldn't be preventing each other
from wandering off. We should enjoy each other, enjoy our kids,
make sure everyone is happy, and also please ourselves separately. It
shouldn't be impossible to do all of those things at once.

I realized that I'd internalized this notion that marriage and
kids and middle age meant you were supposed to shut up and disappear politely. I knew I had no interest in doing that. So instead I
became a little bit extra, a little bit ridiculous, very self-indulgent:
taking selfies, tweeting obnoxiously, making absurd TikToks.
Suddenly I didn't care if every last human alive thought I was
a vainglorious show-off. I just *couldn't care*. I would try to care, in
fact, and I couldn't squeeze the concern into my brain. It fell out
like a handful of Jell-O.

I just wanted to follow my desires wherever they led. They were
leading me back to Bill, mostly, but I was also making new friendships and having intensely emotional conversations with everyone,
new friends and old. I struck up a new friendship with a songwriter
in Portland who approached me on Twitter. I became closer with

a TV writer in LA who I kept bumping into at parties. I decided I wanted to get to know more smart, creative people who loved to talk about emotions and ideas the way I did. And it worked. I started to feel much more connected to other people and to the wider world outside. I was an extrovert who'd been living an intro-verted life for way too long. Everything would be different from that point forward. I would make sure of it.

$$\infty$$

Two days before my big Valentine's party, my cell phone rang. It was a woman from the breast-imaging center where I'd had an MRI eight days earlier, a precautionary measure my sister and I took every year because my mom had been diagnosed with breast cancer the year she turned fifty.

"Has your doctor called you yet?" the woman on the phone asked. I said no.

"Do you want me to schedule your biopsy?" she asked. "We only do one of these a day, so the next one isn't for a week."

I was sitting in my car, parked in my driveway. *This is it*, a voice in my head said. *This is the moment everything changes.* The fig tree in the neighbor's yard, where little birds ate breakfast every morn-ing, had been hacked down to a wretched tangle of stubs. What would those little birds eat for breakfast?

"Yes," I said. "Schedule the biopsy."

I am paying for my sins, I thought. *I wanted too much.* Once a Catholic, always Catholic.

I went inside to call my doctor. Her assistant said my doctor was at another office, but she could call me back next Wednesday, the same day as the biopsy. I could feel my pulse start to race. "That is . . . so unacceptable, I don't even know what to say."

"Do you want to talk to someone else here?" she asked.

"Uh, yes, obviously, unless you want me showing up for a biopsy without knowing what it's for."

A few minutes later, another doctor in the practice called me back. I told him I was confused about why no one had called me for eight days. "Of course we *all* want doctors to be on call twenty-four/seven," the doctor said, suddenly becoming Principal Skinner, explaining the world to a small, stupid child. "But that's not how it works in reality."

"My sister is a cancer surgeon, so I am familiar with the constraints on health professionals," I said, becoming very calm in that I-will-soon-murder-you-with-my-bare-hands way. "But eight days strikes me as suboptimal, since apparently the report was finished the afternoon of my MRI."

"It can take two days just to have the report show up in our system," the doctor said. "Then it takes another two days . . ."

The room felt enormous. My heart was beating in my ears. I needed real information about whether I was dying or not. I pictured the doctor in his office. I tried to imagine how it would feel to explain systemic delays to a stranger who's worried that she might be dying. I wanted to tell him that I could find out the temperature in Chile at that very moment, using only my phone. I wanted to remind him that I could cancel appointments with his office *instantly*, via text. But for some reason, I needed to wait more than a week just to discover that I might have cancer. I wanted to hurt this little man using my words, through the telephone. There should be an app for that.

He was still going on about how many days it took to do things in some caveman era where people sent messages via pterodactyl when I interrupted him. "Can you tell me what's on the report," I said. "Because it's not in the system."

"We don't put these into the system," said the little man on the phone. I almost felt sorry for him.

"Are you looking at the report now?" I asked.

There was a long pause. "The radiologist is simply indicating that further investigation might be necessary." Then he said some other words, but they were all the fact-free, institutional-daddy version of the far scarier words he was reading on the report. You could tell by how many varieties of mild words he was using that there were some seriously ominous words on that document. You could tell that he wasn't sure how bad it was, but that it didn't seem good. It was not a very reassuring form of reassurance.

So I called back and asked the assistant to put the report into the portal so I could read it myself. She said they didn't do that, since in caveman world, cavewomen preferred to wait for weeks for an in-person appointment, just so a condescending Daddy Caveman could describe scary things to them face to face. But she agreed to put the report online nonetheless.

BIRADS-4: SUSPICIOUS. The first part of the report talked about density and fibrosity in both breasts, the radiologist's version of "I can't see shit in here, so don't blame me." Then came the bad part: a linear, segmental, non-mass enhancement with rapid uptake and washout kinetics. I translated this as "We don't know what this is, but you know, it's growing capillaries to feed it like something out of *Invasion of the Body Snatchers*, so that can't be good."

The final portion of the report described my chest and torso as "grossly unremarkable." That's not how *I* would describe my breasts, but okay. It did at least sound like my entire midsection was not yet riddled with tumors.

I spent that evening drinking gin and making jokes about getting my remarkably resilient boobs lopped off. I spent the next day crying my eyes out while the kids were at school, then spent that evening reading research papers and radiology training materials on the morphological characteristics and vascularity of non-mass enhancements. With my family history plus the linear and segmental designations, it looked like I had a 50 percent chance of malignancy. A coin toss.

I called my sister to ask her about it. She said my reasoning sounded solid but warned me not to jump to any conclusions. She said she'd ask some of her colleagues about it and call me back.

When she called back the next day, she told me I was probably right about the 50 percent thing. "Try to think about something else," she said, as if she had never met me before in her life.

$$\infty$$

I spent four days exercising and cleaning the house with my head in a fog. I discovered that it was extremely unpleasant to discuss potential negative health outcomes with your friends and family while you were still unsure of the facts. People really love to instruct you not to feel any feelings. They love to warn you against gathering information on your own. They also enjoy reading their own assortment of studies and summaries of studies, so then they can tell you that *they* figure you have only a 20 percent chance of having cancer. "I'm sure it's fine," they'll announce to you in a final way, making it clear that further talk of your fear and anxiety is unwelcome, since having a one in five chance of a deadly disease is just *not a big deal at all.* "I had a bad pap test once," they'll tell you, and you have to suppress the urge to reply, "Yes. Me, too. This is nothing like that. This is much worse."

So I called my friend Helen, who's actually had cancer. I remembered how often I told her everything would be fine, back when she was waiting for a diagnosis. I remembered how often I read studies because she didn't want to read anything. I would give her the broad strokes, and make guesses about what I was reading. At some point after lots of random reading, I started to think that she shouldn't let her regular doctor do the surgery to remove the cyst on her ovary. I told her that if the worst-case scenario happened, it sounded to me like she'd want an experienced cancer surgeon there, staging the tumor (if it was a tumor, which it wasn't, but just in case!). If anything looked messed up, she'd want a specialist making sure the proper cells were sent off to the proper people, to analyze the margins.

Helen wasn't that thrilled to hear this at the time, but she didn't want to look at any information online herself, so I felt like I needed to warn her about how she handled her cyst. After that, she did end up going to a specialist that my sister found for her, and she ended up having cancer, too. She was thankful that she took my not entirely welcome advice and saw a specialist. She also ended up losing her hair and lying around the house crying for months and a whole year of her life was, in her words, "pure shit."

"I get it now," I told her on the phone, staring out my front window at the high school across the street from our house. Maybe I wouldn't even live long enough to see my kids go there. "I remember all of the dumb things I said to you, about how it was stupid to worry about it because it would all be okay."

"You weren't even that bad. You can't talk to most people."

"I don't even know whether I have cancer or not, but I've already told too many people about it," I said. "Now I have to have conversations about a big question mark. It's agonizing. It just makes it worse."

"I know, it's terrible!" Helen said.

That night when I got into bed, my incredibly nice but doomed boobs hurt like crazy. Was that a bad sign? I pictured warring tribes of cells, invading innocent villages of cells. I mentioned this to Bill.

"I know it sucks, but you just can't think about it," he said.

"Good idea, I'll just turn my brain off," I hissed.

My phone buzzed. An acquaintance I didn't know that well was checking in because another friend had told her I was about to get a needle biopsy.

"Fuck, why did I tell *anyone* about this? I should've kept my mouth shut."

"Everyone just cares a lot," Bill said, rubbing my shoulder a little. "So many people love you so much."

"Oh my god, please stop!" I snapped. "I feel like I'm attending my own funeral, and we don't even know anything yet."

"Jesus," Bill said, pulling his hand away.

"I'm sorry, but you don't understand how alienating it is to be where I am! The last thing I want is to picture other people worrying about me. I don't *care* about anyone else right now. There's just me and death. I'm in this alone."

"That's not true."

"Well, that's how it feels right now. Let me be where I am, for fuck's sake."

So we both got quiet. All we could do was lie in bed, silently feeling bad. And I used to think that people who freaked out while waiting for the results of a health test were so overdramatic. Now I understood. Your brain tried on all of the possibilities, ranging from sickness to death. How could you not? You started to mourn your old life before it was even over.

And in the middle of this despairing state, you also had to field calls and texts. Everyone was so solemn, but you had to agree that you'd be fine or you were hurting *them* somehow. So few people were capable of asking you how you were feeling or what you were thinking when the stakes were high. No one could handle the unknown.

Reassurance isn't reassuring when no one knows anything. Comfort isn't comforting when you're on an island in the middle of a vast ocean. In the middle of the ocean, you *know* you're doomed. You're the only one who knows.

Bill started rubbing my back again without saying anything. Two people grow old together, but maybe only one of them survives. Two people hope to survive together. The world narrows to one boat on the ocean. I had to cancel the party.

Remember? I was going to have a party.

When I canceled, a friend wrote back, "Coronavirus?" We had both been watching from a distance as the mysterious illness spread from China to Italy.

"Possible cancer," I wrote back. It's almost like I wanted to shock him, to make him feel as bad as I felt. It's almost like I wanted to crowd everyone onto the boat in the middle of the ocean with me, until it sank and we all drowned together. At least that way I wouldn't be alone.

Sometimes words are the least helpful thing. Sometimes silence is much better. As I waited for my test results, I went from laughing to crying to mumbling to not talking at all. Instead of talking, I woke up early and wrote. The blank page understood me. Behind the blue sky, invisible stars were twinkling in the vacuum of space. Beyond the horizon, the ocean was rising. We were all doomed. Only a few of us realized it.

18

Plague

The call from the doctor came as I was walking the dogs: No cancer! They found a high-risk lesion called ALH. It would have to be surgically removed, but it wasn't a big deal. Bill and I celebrated. We called everyone to tell them the good news.

Then I met with a breast surgeon, who explained that when they removed the lesion, they'd take a wider excision, just in case.

"So, you're *still* looking for cancer?" I asked.

"Yes," she said, without reassuring me that it was unlikely that they'd find anything. "We just need to see if anything else is there."

"But . . . some kinds of breast cancer are very small and pretty scattered, right? So you might not be totally sure, even after this operation."

"Right," she said, and looked at me without speaking. Imagine being able to stop right there, after all the terrible things you've seen. Imagine not launching into a monologue about the countless patients who got the invisible, scattered kinds of cancer and then *died*, right in front of your eyes, year after year, and there just wasn't much you could do about it. Such restraint!

"So you're just taking a smallish amount," I said. I pictured a small sphere removed from my breast. "Like a melon ball?"

Doctors usually hate me, for reasons that should be apparent by now. But the surgeon laughed. Her laugh told me that everything would be fine. It wasn't until much later that I realized she just happened to be one of the only doctors I'd ever met who had a great sense of humor.

I rescheduled my party for early March. Surgery would happen in late March. Everything was back on track.

We'd dodged a bullet. The apocalypse had been postponed. The gods were on my side again.

$$\infty$$

On February 29, the first American citizen was reported to have died of the coronavirus. On March 6, I canceled my party again. People wrote back to tell me I was being neurotic. By the end of the following week, public schools in Los Angeles were closed.

I had been following the news of this pandemic since mid-January, worried by reports that this strange virus was spreading asymptomatically. It seemed particularly unsettling that it sometimes took as much as two weeks for symptoms to show up, after exposure. So I started to stock up on extra food and surgical gloves and a family pack of Wet Ones and some big jugs of rubbing alcohol.

I was worried that Bill would get very sick if he caught the virus. He always got a terrible cough whenever he caught a cold. I was also worried that my daughter's asthma counted as a comorbidity. I was worried that the hospital would cancel my surgery. Maybe they'd be unprepared for the virus and become overwhelmed with a surge of sick people. I tried to get an earlier surgery date, but nothing was available.

The surgeon finally called a week before my surgery was scheduled. I was at Ivy's asthma doctor's office, taking her for her allergy shots, which couldn't be skipped. "We have to reschedule your surgery," the surgeon said. "The hospital is running out of masks."

Ivy had just had her shot, and we were waiting to make sure she didn't have an allergic reaction. She looked upset. She was clutching the arms of her chair, but she didn't have any gloves on. "Don't touch that," I said to her, my voice muffled through my mask. "Don't touch anything."

I handed her a Wet One from the pack I'd brought along. The surgeon gave me a new date, six weeks later. I thanked the surgeon and hung up, but there was no chance I'd have surgery that soon. Everything would stay shut down, and I'd have to worry about some invisible cancer growing for months on end. Who knew what was in there? My breasts were two dirty bombs, ready to go off at any second.

Ivy suddenly had a red blotch on her face. She was trying not to cry. I'd forgotten to have her take a Zyrtec before her shots, so she'd just had one at the office and it wasn't working yet.

So we sat there in the waiting room, together, trying not to cry. It was hard to grasp that we were in the middle of a global crisis. Seeing everyone in masks felt surreal. It was like everyone on the planet was trying not to cry, together.

On the way home, a lighted sign at the side of the freeway said:

SOCIAL DISTANCING WORKS.
LET'S BEAT COVID-19!

The world is still treating this as a game, I thought. No one realizes how far out to sea we are. No one recognizes that we're all about to drown.

∞

Because my surgery was delayed, my cancer surgeon agreed to put me on a low dose of tamoxifen in order to slow down whatever (entirely theoretical) cancer could be lurking in my chest, which hurt all the time now. Was I in pain because I was being invaded by cancerous cells, or because I was taking a drug that shut down the estrogen receptors in my breast cells? I couldn't be sure, but the sensation was unsettling.

Even though I knew that the cancer, if there was any, would probably be discovered early, I still hated waiting indefinitely to find out more. And I still felt very sorry for myself. It was truly suboptimal to start taking tamoxifen in the middle of a global pandemic. Tamoxifen blocks the effects of estrogen in the breast tissue, which slows down or stops all cancers that are estrogen-receptor-positive. I'd always sort of assumed that estrogen was the friendly chemical provocateur that made me feel like a horny teenager for a solid year, and also woke me up early to write five thousand words every other day, and maybe even kept me looking youthful and giving me energy.

I was right about that, apparently. Because once I started taking tamoxifen, I did not feel smart or pretty or horny or youthful. The luminous goddess had transformed into an angry bridge troll with bad acne and aching knees and a growing sense of anxious dread and claustrophobia. And just as these symptoms really came to a head, Zeke and his girlfriend came to live with us for a month.

Thankfully, we have a big house. The suburbs made that possible. And it didn't seem like such a bad choice once Zeke moved upstairs. Even so, there were six of us. Now every room seemed to have at least one person in it. That person was usually either watching something on TikTok without headphones or talking loudly on the phone or playing Zelda while discussing how to solve the little complexities of Zelda. These were normally things I enjoyed witnessing. Before tamoxifen, I enjoyed fun in general. Before the global pandemic, I had a robust sense of humor.

On tamoxifen during a global pandemic, trapped with several loud humans and animals in the same house for weeks on end, surrounded by meals to be made and dishes to be done and floors to be vacuumed and approximately six extra-large dependents who rarely completed a single one of these tasks without being instructed to do so, I became a hissing opossum lady.

Internally, that is. On the outside, I stayed quiet. I loved these dependents and they needed each other, and us, to help them through this nightmarish time. We played Monopoly. I lost a lot, not because I threw the game, but because I cared less about winning than before, plus I liked watching the kids win. Zeke is a vegetarian, so we started making vegetable dishes using fresh herbs from my rapidly expanding driveway garden. Bill baked a lot of bread. We tried to exercise more than usual. That helped the most.

But then one night, the wheels came off. Bill was playing Zelda, too. He seemed to be staging some kind of a protest because he'd made dinner three nights in a row. He'd stepped up because I was still out of sorts and adjusting to my medication. But now it was clearly my turn to make dinner.

I got up and went into the kitchen, trying to rally myself to find something to make. But when I looked around at the sink full of dishes and the counters covered in more dishes and spills and crumbs, and I heard the sound of Zelda and Zelda play-by-play commentary, I felt ill. All I wanted to do was lie down on the kitchen floor and cry.

Normally, I can just push through this kind of a mood. Yeah, sure, you're not in the mood to make dinner. *But dinner must be made.*

Not this time. I couldn't think straight. I started to sweat and panic. Did I mention that tamoxifen gave me hot flashes? I didn't know what to do with myself. I couldn't move. I wanted to cry. I knew that wouldn't help. I was probably slowly dying of cancer and my last days would be spent like this: trapped, cooking and cleaning around the clock.

"Hey Bill," I said. "Could you come hang out with me in the bedroom for a second?"

Bill was often pretty clueless about tone when we first got married, but now he had a very sensitive radar that could pick up one of my future meltdowns from a room or two away. He got up off the couch immediately. Nobody noticed. My husband was like a dog who could hear a special pitch that no one else could register.

We went back to the bedroom, and I sat on the bed.

"I need your help," I said. I congratulated myself inside my head for making such a neutral but direct statement.

"What do you want me to do?" Bill was already impatient. He could tell I was freaking out, but he wanted to get back to Zelda. He didn't want to do this. *Of course* I couldn't deal, on his first night off!

"Listen to me," I said. "It's a miracle that I'm not throwing things or crying right now. Sit down, please. I need to talk for a second to keep myself from yelling at someone."

"Okay." Bill sat down on the side of the bed.

"I don't know how to fix this. I need your help. I can't listen to that game anymore, but I really need to not be an asshole about it. I don't want these kids to feel bad. They feel bad enough as it is. I need to protect them from me. I need *your help* to protect *them* from *me*."

"Okay, baby. I get it," Bill said.

"Let me finish!" I said. Every sensation was an offense. "No, I mean, sorry, I mean, thank you. I'm just, I'm *sorry*, I just can barely . . . okay. I just need to sit here for a minute and talk to you."

Bill put his hand on my knee and rubbed it. It didn't feel good. Everything chafed. I was like an amoeba in a petri dish filled with acid. Everything made everything worse.

Bill stopped moving his hand, but (miraculously) did not remove it from my knee. Such restraint! This charitable act gave me the strength to speak.

"I'm sorry," I said. "But everything is very bad. And I've been very good about how *bad* everything is. I haven't been a dick about anything, really, considering how shitty I feel."

"I know. You've been really good."

"Don't talk for a second. The point is, I can't be this good all the time. It's impossible. I haven't let myself *feel* anything. I have been holding my fucking breath. It's so important that I not lose my shit right now, around the kids."

"They can take it."

"I don't know if *I* can take it. But right now I need to get this right. I can't go off."

"I get it, but . . . it's hard. Today I saw dishes everywhere, and I almost just started breaking things. It doesn't matter how many times we tell them."

"I know. But I was like that at their age. I think we just need to make some rules, like don't talk on the phone in the living room or play Zelda on the big TV when you're the only one playing."

"That's a good idea."

"But I can't tell them that right now, because my tone will be too harsh. I have to wait."

"Yes, I agree."

Bill is so good. He really is. This conversation was so necessary for me at that moment. Bill was also exhausted and stressed out, but he could tell I had hit the wall.

I had been high on life, and suddenly I was in a dark cave underground.

Bill helped me put the wheels back on. We returned to the living room, and I felt okay. I wasn't alone. Bill understood how it felt under my skin. That's all I really needed, as it turned out. That's all I ever need most of the time. Even as everything else is falling apart.

Locked in, we're forced to look at what we have. Who remembers how to love in close quarters? Look at this square of land and these animals, these humans and this sunny garden. Who will help you when you desperately need help?

"We have more than most," Bill said at dinner that night.

"We're lucky," my older daughter said.

"Things are about to get much worse," I said. My daughter's face fell, but I meant it as a prayer, as a blessing, as a nod toward the inevitable, as a comfort.

I meant: *We can survive this. Open your eyes and look. What do you have? Can you stay right here and appreciate everything that's here?*

∞

"How do we live here together, just us, all alone, indefinitely? Will this end soon, or will we be forced to live this way until we're dead in the ground?" These are the questions that plague you whether you're married or you're just enduring an unprecedented global pandemic.

If you're married *and* you're enduring a global pandemic, well, then, you're plagued by multiple plagues at once. The plague of the actual plague, of course, which is frightening and mysterious and just might kill you. And the plague of your spouse, who is not only growing older and crustier and arguably more annoying by the minute, right in front of your eyes, but who also never seems to leave. He never *seems* to leave because *he never actually leaves*. He is right there, within spitting distance, around the clock.

But as the weeks and the months rolled along, Bill didn't look the same to me anymore. He didn't look old and crusty, and he didn't even seem to make bad sounds anymore. Or if he was making them, I didn't notice them as much. It wasn't just that he was making half of the meals and doing half of the dishes and talking to the kids and walking the dogs every single day. It wasn't just that he let me write every morning and tolerated it when I said things like "Fuck cooking, let's order a pizza. I feel lazy."

Bill looked different and felt different because *we* were different. When he walked into the room, I didn't feel crowded the way I'd been feeling for a while—ironic, really, since now we were trapped inside together, all the time. I found myself moving toward him, instead of moving away.

I felt more patient and accepting of all of us. After spending almost a year trying to untangle my own giant knot of buried desires and insecurities and fears, I became more forgiving of everyone else's quirks. I found myself wanting to make sure that everyone in the family could show their truest selves, and express their emotions, and understand their own needs, without feeling ashamed of who they were.

I bought a bunch of cookbooks, and Bill and I started to work our way through them, planning meals together, talking about who should make what. We always spent a lot of time together, but now, even though we couldn't leave the house, we were enjoying each other's company a lot more.

∞

In May, I finally went in for my surgery. They had to place a wire in my breast first, guided by an MRI. The procedure lasted two hours because the MRI machine had to be rebooted three times. (Two full hours without moving an inch, with my boob in a vise. Can you imagine? Please go ahead and imagine it, because it was medieval.) The pathologist examined the tissue from the lumpectomy and found invasive lobular cancer—just one millimeter of it. It was a miraculous discovery, when you look at it from the right angle. I had caught it as early as you can.

When my surgeon called to tell me the bad news, I was calm. Thanks to my mom's cancer, I'd spent decades anticipating that I'd have to deal with this possibility at some point. I no longer had to worry that my cancer would grow invisibly and then kill me out of the blue. Instead, what felt like a death sentence a few months earlier now felt like a best-case scenario.

I still feel lucky now. But I have no idea how lucky I actually am. That's how life is. Your luck is always inherently temporary, because no one knows what comes next.

I've always known that Bill was my closest friend and favorite person, the only human being I'd ever told everything to, but I had spent a few years trying to keep him at arm's length without realizing it. It's hard to depend on the same person for years. It makes you feel vulnerable.

My love had started to take the shape of sleepwalking. I had subconsciously begun to believe that the only way to hold my marriage together was by barely knowing how I felt or how Bill felt. I had turned the volume down on him and on myself without realizing it.

At some point, tuning in to my desires had started to feel threatening. Maybe that was some creeping realization that we had limited time left. I didn't want to acknowledge how high the stakes felt now. What if our lives changed? What if Bill died or I died? Welcoming whatever Bill wanted seemed dangerous, too. How could two people stay together when they both wanted so much?

But now our needs and fantasies didn't feel threatening or contradictory. Even though the world felt scarier than ever, our needs felt like they were naturally aligned. We both wanted more from our marriage, from ourselves, from each other. And that felt good. It felt *great* to surrender to how much we wanted.

In the middle of the coronavirus pandemic, somewhat ironically, I stopped feeling trapped. Or maybe I decided that out of all the traps out there, I like this trap the best.

∞

A few months into the pandemic, I wrote a letter to an imagined reader, someone who refused to connect with other people, someone who kept backing away and holding the whole world at bay. When I reread it that fall, it struck me that I had been writing to myself, about Bill:

> *You will feel misaligned with your purpose on this earth as long as you ignore your opponent, your imaginary friend, your patron, your padawan, your dragon hiding in the mountain, your rusty wrench, your master, your fidget spinner, your inspiration, your servant, your patient garden, your rising tide, your dirty bomb, your falling star.*

19

Ending

I woke up this morning and rolled over and rubbed Bill's back. I noticed the tiny black hairs springing out of his shoulders like alfalfa sprouts, and briefly considered whether or not it would be smart to take a clipper to them. Maybe the stubble would be worse than the sprouts.

I squeezed his shoulders, meaty from doing a lot of push-ups in quarantine for almost a year now. *We're just two meaty animals, aging rapidly, suspended in memory foam like woolly mammoths,* I thought. *Our fate is to decompose here, slowly, night after night, waiting for our memories to fail, waiting to go blind, waiting to stop tasting and smelling and feeling good, waiting to stop having sex, to stop talking, falling silent, cells breaking down, chemical decomposition already beginning.*

That didn't seem sad for some reason. Too many months in the same house together have turned me into the human version of a haunted mine, creepily addicted to darkness and longing. I rolled through some dirty scenarios inside my head and chose one, trusting that the woolly mammoth next to me would comply. It felt important to have sex often in the final milliseconds of our lives together as fully functioning animals. Sex also felt like a crucial way of staving off pandemic dread.

Later, Bill drank his coffee and I drank my tea and we looked through our cookbooks and ordered groceries for the week. Then Bill started making phlegmy sounds and I told him he should drink more water for the fifty thousandth time and then he snorted and I told him he should blow his nose for the sixty millionth time and he said "I blew my nose this morning!" like he deserved a pat on the back for that. I didn't feel irritated. We were just making our usual noises at each other, not really believing that either of us was capable of change, just reasserting our differences of opinion like two caged birds, cawing at each other just to pass the time.

I sat back on the couch with my cup of tea on my chest and studied Bill, reading something on his laptop: black T-shirt, big hands, messy brown hair looking long and faintly French thanks to the pandemic lockdown. *He's sexy even when he's just sitting there*, I thought. I wondered if I was really good enough for him for the fifteen millionth time. I decided I was charming enough to be worth it but also a little gross for the twenty billionth time.

"You know what my curse in life is?" I asked him. "Deciding if you're good or bad and deciding if *I'm* good or bad, over and over again, every single day."

"That's very true," Bill said. "That's *exactly* what you do. And I'm happy to say that I don't do that at all, ever."

"No, your idea of me doesn't change."

"My high opinion of you was locked in years ago, and it just gets more chiseled in stone."

"I could sprout tentacles and you'd be like 'Oh, this is new! I *like* this.'"

But I have to admit, I enjoy reworking the same equations over and over again like some kind of sudoku addict. That said, when I look back at 2020, I won't just think, *That was the year of the pandemic, the year I got cancer, the year I tried to make my life bigger and it got smaller instead.* I'll also think that it was the year I learned how to etch a fixed idea of my husband in stone, to recognize how much I love him without moving away from that feeling repeatedly, just because it scared me.

It takes work sometimes, to love the people you trust, and to trust the people you love. I didn't grow up that way. I was always worried everyone around me was about to leave: my father, my mother, my brother, my sister. I was holding my breath, waiting for the sky to fall. When I look at Bill now, I no longer see him as someone with special impairments that make him the only man on earth who could ever put up with me. That was part of my bad storytelling, a distortion in my own lens, a projection of my own fears. And even underneath my conviction that he'd never leave me was this archaic fear that everyone *always* left, that no one could be trusted, that no love was dependable and solid.

I look at Bill now, and I can see not just that he'll stay, but that he *wants* to be here. He doesn't just love me unconditionally, and as a result, he's trapped here forever. He hears my weird cawing from across the icy tundra and it sounds melodious to his ears. I haven't tricked him into this. All I've ever done is tell him the truth, and through some miracle, the truth is what Bill craves the most.

Bill is both the parent and the best friend I've always wanted and never had. It feels almost unbearably vulnerable to admit that.

And yes, I need him, but that's not the whole picture. I've always been able to admit that I needed him, that he was propping me up in every way, giving me the impression that I could swim without trying, making me believe that every new tentacle I sprouted was beautiful. What I've had trouble admitting was that we actually *wanted* each other day after day. We weren't just begrudgingly going along with some vow we made years ago. We were choosing each other every morning, all over again, exercising our free will, just like the most clichéd wedding vows always say. I had to do some complicated math, and all Bill had to do was go back to his stone tablets and reread them, but the outcome was the same: we were *both* fully invested—invested in each other's wildest needs and desires, invested in the whole truth, invested in our love for each other, and invested in our life together, trying to make it as good as it could possibly be.

But I've still struggled to stand still and *feel* his love for me. It's the hardest thing to do, sometimes: just to stand still and be loved.

∞

Bill shares a birthday with Queen Elizabeth II. My daughter pointed this out to me the other night when we were all watching *The Crown.* Like the queen, Bill is a firmly grounded but slightly stodgy Taurus, stubborn but also anxious to please, anxious to help. I don't really believe in astrology, but the more I watch *The Crown,* the more sense it makes. Like Queen Elizabeth, Bill looks rigid from the outside sometimes, so his sense of humor is a surprise. But underneath his diplomatic, conventional exterior, he's a tenacious contrarian. He's also the most deeply egalitarian man

I've ever met, utterly committed to fairness in every dimension of his life. Whenever I place our domestic responsibilities against the backdrop of what our sexist hell world expects of me, Bill rips up our previous plan and reshapes it to make it more fair.

As much as I hate to admit it, a big part of my ability to think of myself as free and powerful and unbounded by the humiliations of the wider culture was created inside the bubble of our lives together, where my thoughts and feelings and opinions are welcomed without prejudice. Unlike the wider world outside our door, Bill likes to hear all of the words that come tumbling out of my face. He doesn't worry that I might be smarter than him. He'd prefer that, actually.

I'm hopelessly competitive, so *I'd* prefer it, too. I'm a Gemini, just like Prince Philip. Once my daughter told me this, I couldn't stop noticing my similarities to Philip, or at least to his character on the show. He's basically a prick. He spends the first half of their lives together pacing and looking around for new sources of amusement and distraction and titillation while the Queen carries out her far more honorable tasks.

Prince Philip craves excitement, but he also looks at the big picture more than Queen Elizabeth does. The Queen makes choices based on what aligns with the needs of the motherland, and what serves the greater good. She goes back to first principles: *I am the head of the Church of England, a duty I don't take lightly.*

But she also asks questions at the breakfast table like, "Who is Billy Joelle?"

Philip suppresses a laugh. "Uptown Girl?" he offers, through a smirk.

"What are you talking about?" the Queen replies.

In one of the best episodes of *The Crown*, Philip gets obsessed with the moon landing, obsessed with adventure and men who get to go places and do things, unlike him. He's invited to talk to the new dean of Windsor, who has started a group for retired pastors. Philip shows up and calls them all pathetic to their faces. He says that what *he* cares about are *men of action*.

Then Philip meets the actual astronauts, fresh from the moon landing, and they're a huge disappointment: chuckling, fidgeting, devoid of insights into what they've just accomplished. So he goes back to the dean and the retired pastors, and he apologizes for being such a jerk. He says he's felt restless, dissatisfied. He's been exercising compulsively, searching for more from his life. He admits that he's having a crisis, but "I don't want to say what kind of a crisis." Then he shifts into a softer place: "My mother died recently. She saw that something was missing in her youngest child, her only son. Faith. 'How's your faith?' she asked me. I'm here to admit to you that I've lost it. And without it, what is there?"

Like me, Philip is the kind of person who evaluates whether the Queen is good or bad and whether he himself is good or bad every day. Some days all he can see are those wisps of starchy white hair at the sides of her head, or the way she purses her lips right before she's about to ring the bell that says, *Take this visitor away before we talk about anything substantive.* Philip observes more closely than the Queen does, but he's also an ingrate. He's in touch with his desires, and he's impatient for more.

Those sorts of traits can erode your faith, but they don't have to. Longing isn't necessarily the enemy. Just as dreaming of men of action sometimes leads you back to the men of reflection you unknowingly prefer, fixating on the things you can't have before you die sometimes leads you back to the fact that you *already* chose wisely, and everything you're craving is actually within reach.

When you're out of faith, it takes a little patience to recognize that what you have is what you've wanted all along. It also takes some courage to reach for what you want, and to admit to the person who you love the most that you love him the most. It feels frightening. It feels like surrender.

∞

Every book about death is also a book about how to survive in the face of death—which means that every book about marriage is actually a book about survival, and about trying to find happiness together in spite of the fact that you're doomed to fail from the start. You're doomed because even though you're aiming for forever, forever doesn't really exist. You either die or your marriage does. There is no forever.

That's why trying to have a good marriage often feels like trying to believe in something imaginary. You're engaged in this absurd charade together. You're trying to believe that forever is real. You're trying to have faith that somehow, two people can evade death forever, or at least they can evade death for a long time and then *finally die together, hand in hand.* Victory at last!

Only an optimistic fool would declare victory before reaching the finish line. But what is a wedding, if not a celebration of two optimistic fools whose foolish optimism *matches* each other's?

"I worry about the state of your marriage," my mom said to me, thirteen years ago. At the time, I thought she'd rather worry than look at what was right in front of her. But maybe she was only trying to say that no one knows what comes next. Maybe she was trying to tell me that you shouldn't pretend to know everything, because you just don't know. No one does. *No one can predict what happens from here.*

I agree with her now. Nothing is certain. But along with my overly critical mind and my disobedient imagination and my tireless theorems, I have faith now. Even though I know that love is an act of imagination fueled by fear, and marriage is a slowly unfolding apocalypse, I realize that I've found an optimistic fool whose optimism and foolishness match my own. Together, every day, we dare to imagine the impossible. We dare to imagine remaining eternally satisfied. We look into each other's eyes and we see infinity.

And if Bill ever left me, I'd assume that he'd probably come back eventually. If I ever left Bill, he could feel sure that I'd come back. Why wouldn't I? What we have is way too good to give up permanently. My cells are loyal patriots to his microbiome. My heart is aligned with his stubborn pulse. I want for him exactly what I want for myself. Whatever he needs goes straight to the top of my list without hesitation. There's a sickness and a danger to loving and trusting someone this much. It's like handing someone your liver and hoping they don't drop it. The stakes are so high, *too* high, unbearable, excruciating. That also makes it dirty and sick and perfect.

And when the end comes, no matter what, it will be happy. I'll feel in every cell how lucky I was, how lucky we were, to have found each other.

Just don't think for a second that you'll only know that my marriage was happy if we make it to that morbid finish line. You shouldn't need to stay tuned to the very end just to know whether or not we were truly good together. Plenty of great couples fall apart every day. Plenty of shitty couples last to the bitter end. Lots of very lovely people cheat on each other and disappoint each other and break up and get back together and make a mess of a million things together, like a two-headed monster, like a curse, like a dragon and a thief, like a patient garden and a falling star. Sometimes we fail and fumble simply because we're here to feel as much as we can before our time runs out. Bill will still be the love of my life, even if he leaves me tomorrow. I'll still know how it feels to grow tentacles and be loved deeply anyway. *This* is the moment that defines us—you, me, and everyone else—not the end. Is your heart wide open? Are you loved? Can you stand still and feel it?

I want to keep feeling it with every cell of my body. There is nothing better on the face of the earth. The tides can rise and pull us out to sea, but our love won't die. That's not a leap of faith, it is faith itself. It's already chiseled in stone.

ACKNOWLEDGMENTS

Thank you to Sarah Burnes, who changed my career the way a good marriage changes your life. She has encouraged me and stood behind me at every turn, and I hope and pray I can keep her forever.

Big thanks to Sara Birmingham and Denise Oswald at Ecco for shaping this book so thoughtfully and patiently. I owe them both a huge debt of gratitude for their close attention, their incredibly smart edits, and their support. Thank you also to Dan Halpern, Miriam Parker, Helen Atsma, Jonathan Burnham, Meghan Deans, Caitlin Mulrooney-Lyski, and everyone at Ecco for embracing this book so unreservedly.

It was a long, grueling year and so many smart writers and thinkers lent me their time and expertise. Special thanks to Stella Bugbee, Emily Gould, Tracy McMillan, Diane Sawyer, Alana Levinson, Leslie Jamison, Dave Bazan, Lauren Hough, Ken Layne, Ben Smith, Steve Coulter, Niela Orr, Hamish McKenzie, and Ann Friedman for their creative insights and professional guidance. Eternal gratitude to Brendan Maze, Erin Johnson, Jeff Solomon,

Molli McIlvaine, Heather Varnell, Kim Thigpen, Os Tyler, Shannon Hunt, Justin Fisher, and Charlie Hornberger for your wild enthusiasm and calamitous love. And extra-special thanks to Viva de Vicq, a brilliant light who made our lives so much more joyful during a dark time.

Thank you to Perri and Carter Kersh for making marriage look fun and hilarious even when the wheels are coming off. Thanks to Laura Havrilesky, Eric Havrilesky, Jeff Welch, and Melissa Hernandez for always showing up for the chaos of family with a good attitude. Huge thanks to Zeke Sandoval for his big heart, unwavering principles, and unbridled enthusiasm for Wingspan.

My deepest love and gratitude go out to my lifelong sister-wives: Steve Lavine, Kelly Atkins, Andrea Russell, Carina Chocano, and Apryl Lundsten.

Love and thanks to my mother, Susan Havrilesky, who is generous and funny and very good company. I love you and I depend on you more than ever. Thank you to Ivy and Claire for being open-hearted and delightful and committed to kindness and fairness, every single day.

When I set out to write this book, I had no idea how much patience, tolerance, and faith in our relationship would be demanded of my husband, Bill Sandoval. Somehow he never wavered, reading each new draft with more enthusiasm than he read the last. Bill, you're my favorite person in the world. Thanks for showing me how to love and be loved.